# True Secrets of Alaska Revealed!

Cover design by: Greg Needham | Greg Needham Design & Graphics

FIRST EDITION

Inquiries should be addressed to:

Eden Entertainment Limited, Inc.
1107 Key Plaza #195
Key West, Florida  33040

www.TrueSecretsOf.com

LIBRARY OF CONGRESS
CATALOGING IN PUBLICATION DATA

       **Eden Entertainment Limited, Inc.**
       True Secrets of Alaska Revealed!
       First Edition

Printed in the United States of America

**On the Cover:**

Igloo ................................................................. Page 33

Bishop's Boots ................................................ Page 48
(Photo Courtesy Anchorage Museum of History and Art, All Rights Reserved)

Guardian Angel of America Ice Sculpture ........ Page 67

Gold Dredge ..................................................... Page 52

# About The Authors

**Carol Varner** loved dressing up like a Gypsy when she was young. When she grew up she became one. Traveling so much she's made a career of Learning Experiences, that includes sixteen plus jobs, some paid, some not.

After several years as a "camp follower" Carol has settled in North Pole, Alaska, where she contemplates retirement. The only reason she hasn't is it might be too much work and she wouldn't get paid for it.

Until that day she continues opening her mind to understanding through reading and research for Eden Entertainment. It definitely doesn't pay very well but gives her heart a reason to keep beating.

**Daniel "I'm Cold" Reynen** fell in love with the spectacular beauty of Alaska. Immense mountains, virgin forests and wildlife around every corner. While visiting he experienced "life at 30 below." He learned how to deal with ice fog, drive a snowmachine and the value of bunny boots.

Perhaps the most difficult thing for Daniel was the realization he would have to relax his sense of style when he discovered it was almost impossible to coordinate five layers of clothing before going out.

Daniel enjoyed his trips north so much he has made it a regular destination...but mostly during the summer months.

**Marshall Stone** continues his travels by leaving the sands of Florida for the rocky outcroppings of the Olympic Pensinula in Washington State. He has been watching the leaves turn and is enjoying the reassuring odours of the wood-stove. He has put his short breeches away for the season and is learning how to avoid the potentionally foggy humours of a northern winter.

Through the miracle of the computer he continues his feeble contributions to the written word of Eden Entertainment, Ltd. and he hopes you will enjoy Edens' *Alaska* book!

# About The Authors

**Scott Gutelius** made most of his contributions from a heavily climate-controlled environment. Normally, he's in favor of hands-on research, but we all have limits (like frostbite). Yes, he is a whimp. Last we heard he was in Key West playing moose nugget jokes on all his friends. "Wanna hold my tie-tac?"

**Marcus Varner** first moved to North Pole, Alaska in 1983 to experience the last frontier. Striving to educate himself he became a proud dropout of the University of Alaska Fairbanks and decided to make his fortune looking for gold.

Mining was the hardest work he had ever done, but at least he wasn't paid very well. Realizing he had to work hard *and* be lucky Marcus decided to explore Alaska.

In Anchorage he perfected the phrase "fries with that?" and in Juneau he mastered "fish with that?" Years of Alaska living, volcanic eruptions, earthquakes, snow and rain left their mark on Mr. Varner. He'd like to share some of the more unusual tidbits with you in this twisted little book.

# Coming soon...

## True Secrets of Washington D.C. Revealed!

## True Secrets of New Orleans Revealed!

# Available now...

## True Secrets of Key West Revealed!

## True Secrets of Salt Lake City and The Great Salt Lake Revealed!

# Contents

# Early History

## When was Alaska first inhabited?

Nobody knows when the first humans entered Alaska. The best available evidence suggests that the first people walked across a land bridge from Asia at least 20,000 to 30,000 years ago.

The theory goes that these people were following Ice Age mammals migrating east from Siberia into Alaska searching for food. At the time there was a natural land bridge (called the Bering Land Bridge) that was about 1,000 miles wide. The bridge existed during the Pleistocene Epoch (11,000 to 1.8 million years ago). Today there are 56 miles of stormy water separating Siberia's Chukchi Peninsula from the Seward Peninsula of Alaska.

## How did the Russians get involved in Alaska?

It began with the voyages of Vitus Bering and Alexei Chirikof in 1741. They sailed from Russia's Kamchatka Peninsula in the ships *Saint Peter* and *Saint Paul*. Shortly after sailing south of Kodiak Island, in December of 1741, Bering died from scurvy. Chirikof made it along the coastline as far south as present day Sitka. The Russians met with curious natives and traded for *Bobri Morski* (Sea Otter) pelts. The pelts were highly prized in China and Europe so when Chirikof returned to Moscow, Russia began a full charge to this new land.

The following years saw a great influx of *promyshlenniki* (Russian fur hunters) from Siberia. Many of the *promyshlenniki* were unprepared for the dangerous journey across the turbulent North Pacific waters. They were far from home, in a hostile northern climate, living off the land. Grand ideas of easy wealth were quickly abandoned.

## What happened to the first Russians?

The Tsar of Russia stepped in to put things in order. In 1789 Gregor Shelikof was awarded a State Charter by the Tsar and he founded the Rossiisko-Amerikanskoi Kompanii (RAK) known to Americans as the Russian American Company.

Alexander Baronof became the head of the new company and with Russian imperial backing the pillaging of Alaska began.

*Alexander Baronof. Photo taken by permission at the University of Alaska Museum in Fairbanks.*

## But didn't the British also explore Alaska?

Sure did. Captain James Cook of the ship H.M.S. *Resolution* sailed to Alaska from Hawaii in 1778. He landed first on the coastline of present day British Columbia and sailed along the coast north to the Arctic Ocean. Along the way he made maps and was looking for the fabled Northwest Passage.

(The Northwest Passage was a theoretical ice-free passage from the Pacific to the Atlantic. Today we know no such passage exists in North America but in the 1700s it was big business looking for it.)

Just a side note: Captain Cook's best cartographer was a young William Bligh...of *Mutiny on the Bounty* notoriety.

*Statue of Captain James Cook in Anchorage overlooking Cook Inlet.*

## What did Lieutenant James King bury near Anchorage?

Captain Cook sent James King to bury a bottle. The bottle, buried under some rocks by the side of a stunted tree, contained papers relevant to taking possession of the land and water near present day Anchorage.

King later wrote of burying the papers "where if it escapes the Indians, in many ages hence it may puzle antiquarians." (Misspelling is in the original.) I guess they didn't consider the Natives who already lived there to have possession of the land…

## Did the Spanish ever explore Alaska?

Only once. In 1790 Don Salvador Fidalgo made a short journey surveying North American coasts as far north as Prince William Sound. He named places from Washington State to Alaska that remain to this day as the sum of Spanish impact on the region. Troubles in the Spanish southern colonies and a lack of resources to compete against the British and Russians in the north kept them out.

So now the British, Russians and increasingly involved Americans were deciding who actually "owned" Alaska and nobody bothered to ask the established native residents.

## Why did the Russians sell Alaska to the United States?

It all began as a species was being wiped out.

The RAK (Russian American Company) had been based on Kodiak Island for ten years. Over that course of time the population of *Bobri Morski* (Sea Otter) was decimated. The shortage became so severe that in 1799 Alexander Baranof, head of the RAK decided to move to a more central location hundreds of miles southwest along the Alaska coast, to the town of Sitka (then called New Archangel).

Unfortunately, the over-hunting continued and for the next 30 years the fur trade declined. Sea Otter pelts were in such demand that hunting parties went as far east as the Pribilof Islands and as far south as Baja California! Older trading posts that weren't producing were gradually abandoned and the grip Russia had on Alaska began to diminish.

In the meantime, the British were strengthening their control on what would later become Canada, and the United States was pushing westward through the 1800s.

In 1825 agreements were reached between the United States, England and Russia to officially limit Russian America's southern border to 54 degrees 40 minutes north latitude, where Alaska's border terminates today.

But things weren't going well in Mother Russia. Tsar Alexander I at the end of the Napoleonic Wars (1805-1815) forbade political dissent and in doing so created angry masses. (It seems like Russia has quite a history of angry masses.)

When Alexander I died in 1825 Tsar Nicholas was equally repressive. By the 1860s Tsar Alexander II emancipated the Russian serfs, but they were set free in a hostile environment of poverty and unemployment. Uncertainty and fear held Russia's ruling class.

In the meantime, advisors returning from Russian America told tales of significant foreign interest. Minerals were discovered and in massive amounts. The RAK could barely afford to feed its people and Russia couldn't afford to send more men or money to develop or supervise the mining of minerals.

Russia couldn't afford news of these mineral wealths to escape or they wouldn't be able to manage the rush of mostly foreign prospectors. In 1863 Russia virtually abandoned its northwestern colony leaving New Archangel and almost 600 Russian citizens in limbo.

Tsar Alexander II then sent an emissary named Baron Edward de Stoeckl to meet with United States representatives in Sitka. Baron Stoeckl spent nearly $200,000 of his personal fortune to "brighten up" the city of Sitka and after wining and dining his visitors he made a powerful sales pitch. Secretary of State William H. Seward got glowing reports back on the incredible "deal" that Russia was giving.

*William H. Seward. Photo used by permission, Alaska State Library - Historical Collections, all rights reserved.*

The United States agreed to purchase the Russian America colony in 1867 for $7.2 million in a deal arranged by Seward. The purchase price worked out to approximately 2.5 cents an acre. Opponents of the purchase called it *Seward's Folly* and referred to the northern territory as *Seward's Ice Box*, *President Johnson's Polar Bear Garden* and even *Walrussia*.

Alaska's wealth of oil, gold, silver, copper, timber, fish and physical beauty have long since justified Seward's judgment. Alaska was neither a state nor a territory and was called "The Department of Alaska," unincorporated U.S. property.

*Check used to purchase Alaska. Photo courtesy of the United States National Archives and Records Administration, all rights reserved.*

**Why was the price $7,200,000 and not $7,000,000 even?**

Remember Baron Edward de Stoeckl? He spent $200,000 of his own money beautifying Sitka to make the sales pitch to the United States representatives. $200,000 was used to repay him and the remaining $7,000,000 went to the Tsar of Russia.

**Who are the "Pioneers of Alaska"?**

It's an organization started on February 20, 1907 with the goal to "unite the old-timers of Alaska and by permanent organization, preserve the names of all early settlers on its rolls; to collect and preserve the incidents of Alaska's literature and history, and to promote the best interest of the Territory."

Men's groups are called "Igloos" and the women's groups are called "Auxiliaries." Membership was originally limited to people who were Alaskan residents prior to January 1, 1901. Now you must be an Alaskan resident for 30 years before you can apply.

# Natural Phenomenon

**How big is Alaska?**

According to the United States Census Bureau *Census 2000*, Alaska is 571,951 square miles. That size makes it more than twice as big as the next largest state. Alaskans like to remind Texans that if they cut Alaska in half, *each half* would still be larger than Texas. (Don't worry Texans, Alaskans still think your collective ego is much larger than Alaska's.) Alaska is one-fifth the size of the combined Lower 48 states.

Alaska has more coastline, approximately 6,640 miles, than the other 49 states *combined*.

*Relative size of Alaska and the contiguous (Lower 48) United States.*

**Is it true Alaska is the *easternmost* part of the North American continent?**

Absolutely. The Aleutian Islands in Alaska are the farthest *west* extension of the North American continent, but the archipelago crosses 180 degrees into *east* longitude making it the *easternmost* extension as well. This gives Alaska bragging rights to three of four points on the compass, northernmost, easternmost and westernmost.

Incidentally, the Aleutian Islands are also the world's longest archipelago (group of small islands).

**What is the coldest temperature ever recorded in Alaska?**

Eighty degrees below zero Fahrenheit on January 23, 1971 at Prospect Creek, north of the Yukon River. That's BEFORE wind chill.

**And the warmest?**

One hundred degrees Fahrenheit at Fort Yukon in 1915. This heat record happens to be the same as Hawaii. April 27, 1931, Pahala, Hawaii was also 100 degrees Fahrenheit.

**What are the tides like?**

Oh, you know, they come and go. Alaska has the second greatest tide range in North America. The tides in the Upper Cook Inlet near Anchorage are 38.9 feet!

**What the heck is the *keck effect*?**

Bending light poles. It seems that during the winter light poles get extremely cold. If the morning sun is strong the poles warm rapidly, causing the sides toward the sun to expand – and bending the poles

*Bending light poles in North Pole, Alaska led to the discovery of the Keck Effect. Yes, they are painted like giant candy canes.*

away from the heat. By late afternoon the poles straighten out as the heat becomes evenly distributed around the poles. The effect was first observed and documented by Jim Keck while driving on the Richardson Highway from Eielson Air Force Base to the town of North Pole. It is now known as the Keck Effect.

**I've heard that Harvard, Dartmouth, Yale, Columbia, Amherst, Radcliffe, Smith, Bryn Mawr, Vassar and Wellesley are in Alaska. What gives?**

They are, but they're glaciers. The railroad magnate Edward H. Harriman in 1899 sponsored a science expedition to Alaska. During the trip the scientists named many of the glaciers after colleges they attended back home. (To learn more about Edward Harriman get our book, True Secrets of Salt Lake City and the Great Salt Lake Revealed!)

*Yale glacier. Photo courtesy Peter Van Dyne, all rights reserved.*

### What is a glacier?

A glacier is a river or fall of ice made of snow that has been compressed and built up over many years (generally centuries). Glaciers currently cover 30,000

square miles or about five percent of Alaska. There are more than 100,000 glaciers in Alaska.

### Are glaciers made up of anything else?

Rocks. That's right, they are also called a rock-debris fan. An active rock glacier is made up of blocky rock with ice in the spaces between the rocks. Several rock glaciers have been observed in the Alaska Range and the Ogilvie Mountains.

*Rock glacier.*

### How fast do glaciers move?

Many less than a foot or two per day, but there are exceptions. The Black Rapids Glacier garnered worldwide attention in 1937 when it advanced spectacularly at rates of up to 200 feet a day. It was feared that the glacier would quickly reach the Richardson Highway, destroy it, and also destroy the historic Black Rapids Roadhouse. A radio announcer was stationed to broadcast the details of the glacier crunching through the building. Unfortunately for the radio audience, it never happened. The Black Rapids Glacier eventually stopped advancing and today is retreating.

### Have surging glaciers ever done anything else?

In June of 1986 the Hubbard Glacier surged hundreds of feet in a few weeks and dammed Russell Fjord. The lake that formed behind the glacier was named Russell Lake and rose four inches daily. Russell Lake eventually reached a depth of more than 80 feet when on October 8, 1986 the Hubbard Glacier ruptured. 3,500,000 cubic feet of water *per second* poured into Disenchantment Bay. This was the largest water discharge in recorded North American *history*.

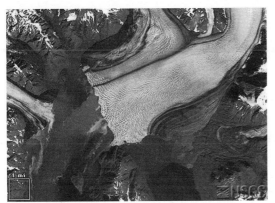

*Hubbard Glacier blocking Russell Fjord in 1986. Photo courtesy United States Geological Survey, all rights reserved.*

### What is the largest glacier in Alaska?

That depends on what type of glacier you are talking about and how you measure them. Alpine glaciers, confined in mountain valleys, are linear rivers of ice. Piedmont glaciers spread out onto plains as sheets of ice.

The largest alpine glacier in North America (and incidentally the longest glacier) is the Bering Glacier complex. It is more than 100 miles long and covers about 2,250 square miles. The largest piedmont

*Malaspina Glacier complex. Photo courtesy National Aeronautics and Space Administration, all rights reserved.*

glacier in North America is the Malaspina Glacier complex, which covers more than 2,000 square miles.

### Is the Malaspina Glacier complex increasing or decreasing in size?

It's actually melting quite a bit. Over the last 20 years Malaspina Glacier has lost the equivalent of 15 cubic miles of water. That's approximately one half of one percent of the total global sea rise during the past 20 years.

### What can you find on page two of the *Fairbanks Daily News-Miner*, but only during the winter?

The Aurora Forecast. A picture showing where the aurora activity will be highest throughout Alaska. The forecast only appears during the winter months because during the summer the sun is out and the aurora isn't visible to the naked eye.

### What is the aurora?

It is a natural phenomenon that appears as a spectacular display of lights dancing across the sky. The aurora borealis goes by many names including the northern lights, flying fires, glowing snakes and even sky dwellers.

In the northern hemisphere the aurora is called the *aurora borealis* while in the southern hemisphere it is called *aurora australis*. Occasionally you will hear *aurora polaris* referring to aurora on both hemispheres.

First called the aurora in 1619 by Galileo Galilei, he named it after the Roman Goddess of Morning, Aurora. Galileo thought the aurora was caused by sunlight reflecting from the atmosphere and used this erroneous observation in an argument against the Roman Catholic Church doctrine that the earth was the center of the solar system (and universe). Galileo was right about earth, but wrong about the aurora.

### What causes the aurora?

The aurora is a result of gases in the upper atmosphere being struck by fast-moving particles coming from the sun.

**Does the aurora sometimes dip down and touch the ground?**

No, it just looks as though it does. The aurora is never lower than 40 miles above the earth's surface but can extend upwards for several hundred miles.

**Have there ever been man-made aurora?**

Well, yes. The first was created over Virginia in 1969 using an electron gun. The gun was placed in the nose cone of a rocket and sent high above most of the atmosphere. The rocket was rotated until it pointed downward along the direction of the earth's magnetic field, then bursts of electrons were shot from the gun. Moving at the speed of nearly 20,000 miles per hour the electrons penetrated the atmosphere, struck the atoms and molecules of the atmosphere and made them glow. The thin streaks of aurora that resulted were too weak to be seen by the unaided eye but they were recorded by sensitive ground-based systems.

*Aurora borealis. Photo courtesy National Oceanic and Atmospheric Administration, photo by Dr. Yohsuke Kamide, Nagoya University and from the Collection of Dr. Herbert Kroehl, NGDC.*

**Does the aurora make any sound?**

None that has ever been proven. Numerous reports exist of people who have "heard" the aurora but so far there is no scientific evidence or recordings to prove it.

**Where is the best place to see the aurora?**

In the auroral zone. It is an elongated belt that encircles the polar regions. The peak of the auroral zone is an imaginary line that statistically offers more auroral activity than any other place on earth. In Alaska three excellent places to view aurora are the towns of Circle, Fairbanks and Fort Yukon.

**When is the best time to see the aurora?**

August 15th to April 15th. This is referred to as the "observing season." During the summer months the aurora is just as active but because the sun is up the aurora can't be seen.

**Are there volcanoes in Alaska?**

Yes, Alaska has more volcanoes than any state *including* Hawaii. There is even one made out of mud, kind of like the one in *Close Encounters of the Third Kind*, but bigger and not built by Richard Dreyfuss.

*Eden Entertainment Researcher Daniel Reynen at the Tolsona Mud Volcano.*

You can walk to the mud volcano from the Tolsona Wilderness Campground on mile 173 of the Glenn Highway. It's actually a warm spring, approximately 25 feet high and as big around as two football fields. At the crest are vents bubbling out methane gas and lukewarm water laced with sodium and calcium chloride.

## What was the largest volcanic eruption in Alaska in the 20th century?

The 1912 eruption of Novarupta in the Katmai group was the largest volcanic eruption *anywhere in the world* for the entire 20th century. It was rated as VEI 6 or colossal. Novarupta erupted seven cubic miles of ash in only 60 hours, covering 46,000 square miles in greater than .40 inches of ash. Pyroclastic flows traveled up to 15 miles and produced the Valley of Ten Thousand Smokes (now a National Park).

R.F. Griggs placed the eruption in perspective:

*"The magnitude of the eruption can perhaps be best realized if one could imagine a similar outburst centered in New York City. All of Greater New York would be buried under from ten to fifteen feet of ash; Philadelphia would be covered by a foot of gray ash and would be in total darkness for sixty hours; Washington and Buffalo would receive a quarter of an inch of ash, with a shorter period of darkness. The sound of the explosion would be heard in Atlanta and St. Louis, and the fumes noticed as far away as Denver, San Antonio, and Jamaica." (Robert F. Griggs, National Geographic Magazine, 1917, v. 81 no. 1, p. 50)*

## How are volcanic eruptions measured?

The Volcanic Explosivity Index or VEI. The VEI is based on height the plume reaches and volume of debris expelled. Below is a table with examples of the VEI range.

| VEI | Description | Plume Height | Volume | Classification | Frequency | Example |
|---|---|---|---|---|---|---|
| 0 | Non-explosive | Less than 100 m | 1000s meters cubed | Hawaiian | Daily | Kilauea |
| 1 | Gentle | 100-1000 m | 10,000s meters cubed | Hawaiian/ Strombolian | Daily | Stromboli |
| 2 | Explosive | 1-5 km | 1,000,000s meters cubed | Strombolian/ Vulcanian | Weekly | Galeras, 1992 |
| 3 | Severe | 3-15 km | 10,000,000s meters cubed | Vulcanian | Yearly | Ruiz, 1985 |
| 4 | Cataclysmic | 10-25 km | 100,000,000s meters cubed | Vulcanian/ Plinian | 10's of Years | Galunggung, 1982 |
| 5 | Paroxysmal | Greater than 25 km | 1 kilometer cubed | Plinian | 100's of Years | Saint Helens, 1981 |
| 6 | Colossal | Greater than 25 km | 10s kilometers cubed | Plinian /Ultra-Plinian | 100's of Years | Krakatau, 1883 |
| 7 | Super-Colossal | Greater than 25 km | 100s kilometers cubed | Ultra-Plinian | 1,000's of Years | Tambora, 1815 |
| 8 | Mega-Colossal | Greater than 25 km | 1,000s kilometers cubed | Ultra-Plinian | 10,000's of Years | Yellowstone |

## What is permafrost?

Permafrost is any soil, subsoil, or other surficial deposit that has a temperature lower than 32 degrees Fahrenheit for at least two years. This definition is based exclusively on temperature. Part or all of the deposit's moisture may be unfrozen, but most permafrost is cemented by ice. Permafrost without ice is called dry permafrost.

Permafrost is a phenomenon of polar, sub polar and alpine regions. About 20 percent of the world's land contains permafrost and an estimated 82 percent of Alaska is underlain by permafrost.

## What is on top of permafrost?

The soil layer overlying permafrost thaws and freezes each year and is called the "active layer."

## Isn't there an alcohol drink called Perma Frost?

Yes. It tastes sort of like drinking mouthwash from a car battery. We like it.

*Yukon Jack® Perma Frost Schnapps.*

## What are pingos?

In scientific terms they are "perennial, conical-shaped ice-cored mounds that are, in exceptional cases, as much as 65 meters high and 1,000 meters in diameter." In un-scientific terms? They are HUGE pimples on the land caused by ice. Some are so large they look like hills.

*Pingo.*

## Can I go inside a pingo?

The only place you once could was in Tuktoyaktuk, Canada. There used to be a "Pingo Tunnel" excavated into the side of a pingo. The tunnel opened into a large room situated beneath the pingo summit. Unfortunately, in July 1979 the tunnel collapsed near the entrance because of thermal erosion along an ice wedge. It was supposedly quite a popular attraction while it was open.

## What is an ice wedge?

A crack is created by the contracting of fine-grained soil masses when the ground temperature falls below about zero degrees Fahrenheit for a long period.

Summer comes along and the crack is filled with water or water molecules during the thaw. When the next cold spell comes along the crack opens again through contraction of the cold ground and expansion of the water freezing. The cycle repeats itself over many years and eventually forms a wedge shape cutting through the soil.

The cracking forms polygon structures on the surface that resemble the shape mud takes when it dries.

## What is an ice wedgie?

Ice wedgies form when the thermal underwear of an Alaskan is yanked suddenly and violently northward by another Alaskan, generally a close and trusted friend.

*Ice wedge polygons as seen from the air. Photo courtesy Chris Ruff, all rights reserved.*

## What is an "explosive icing"?

When the water pressure beneath a frost blister pushes up strongly enough, and if the ice ruptures suddenly, the blister may explode with a loud booming sound. Instances have been recorded where blocks of frozen ground up to six feet thick and 50 feet long have been thrown for considerable distances. Explosive icings have been reported in Interior Alaska and the Brooks Range.

## What is a "bore tide"?

A tide that just wants to talk about itself.

Not really. It's a rushing, one to six-foot high wall of water produced when a strong incoming tide surges into the constricted channel of an inlet. The tide rises up and over water already in the channel. Sort of a wave rushing over water.

One of the best places to see this phenomenon is south of Anchorage near the Seward Highway. The tide occurs when an incoming tide from Cook Inlet heads into the narrow entrance and over the shallower water of Turnagain Arm. The best time to see it is about two hours after low tide in Anchorage.

## What is the tundra?

The treeless expanse that covers much of Alaska and consists of many low-lying, dwarfed plants, mosses and lichen. There is arctic tundra which is low-lying and alpine tundra which is above the treeline. It's a lot like Kansas, but colder. And bigger.

*Tundra.*

## What is the tallest mountain in Alaska?

The official name is McKinley, commonly called Denali and it is North America's tallest mountain at 20,320 feet. (Some measurements show it is only 20,306 feet but what's 14 feet among friends?) However, if you measure a mountain from its base, the highest in the world is Mauna Loa in Hawaii. From the base Mauna Loa rises 32,000 feet. But, the highest *land based* mountain in the world is McKinley. It's even taller than Mount Everest, which only rises 11,000 feet above the Tibetan Plateau.

## Who were the first people to reach the peak of McKinley?

A party led by Episcopal Archdeacon Hudson Stuck first reached the mountain's highest point in 1913. Stuck led Harry Karstens, Walter Harper and Robert

Tatum. Tatum was from Tennessee and the only non-Alaskan in the group. The first woman to reach the peak was Barbara Washburn from Boston, Massachusetts on June 6, 1947.

McKinley is the centerpiece of what used to be called McKinley National Park (named after William McKinley – 25th President-elect of the United States, in 1896 by a miner who liked McKinley's support of the gold standard). The park is now called Denali National Park after the Athabaskan word that means "the great one" or "the high one."

*Mount McKinley. Tallest mountain in North America. Photo courtesy Bob Hammond, all rights reserved.*

**Does McKinley hold any other records?**

North America's deepest gorge. "Great Gorge" is on the south side of Mount McKinley and measures nearly 9,000 feet deep. That's deeper than the Grand Canyon!

The Wickersham Wall on the north face is one of the highest vertical inclines in the world, rising 15,000 feet.

*Great Gorge on Mount McKinley. Photo courtesy Chris Ruff, all rights reserved.*

*Joe Redington, Sr. (standing) and Susan Butcher (seated) on top of McKinley with sled dog team. Photo taken by Robert Stapleton and provided courtesy of Vi Redington from her personal collection, all rights reserved.*

**What was one of the more unusual ascents of McKinley?**

One that was made in the summer of 1979, when 62 year-old Joe Redington, Sr. and Susan Butcher, accompanied by Brian Okonek, Ray Genet and Robert Stapleton, mushed a team of four dogs to the top of the mountain. You read that right. They climbed the highest mountain in North America with a sled and dog team.

To illustrate just how difficult that is, during that year 659 people attempted to climb McKinley but only 283 of them reached the summit. For more information on Joe Redington, Sr. see page 68.

**Is it easy to see Mount McKinley?**

One would think that North America's highest mountain is difficult to miss. On a clear day McKinley is even visible from the city of Fairbanks, 150 miles to the north.

Unfortunately, finding a clear day near McKinley is very difficult. The mountain is so large, it creates its own weather system, so two thirds of the time McKinley is hidden by thick clouds.

It's ironic that the Denali Visitors Center has numerous photographs of Mount McKinley because many tourists who go there can't see the mountain.

## What's it like to climb Mount McKinley?

The best fat farm in the country. Climbers step out of a plane onto the mountain's Kahiltna Glacier and immediately their bodies undergo changes. The camp is at an elevation of 7,000 feet and the thin air makes breathing difficult and increases the body's metabolic rate. A climber sitting down doing nothing burns as many calories as someone exercising at sea level.

At this point the summit is more than 13,306 feet higher. You have to get to the first camp with a 60-pound pack on your back dragging a 40-pound sled while cross-country skiing.

No matter what or how much you eat, you will loose weight. The average is 10 to 20 pounds over a three-week climb with each person burning an average of 5,500 calories every day!

## What do climbers eat to keep from starving?

One of the more famous foods is Hello Dollies (also known as the ultimate gut bomb). The following is Stuart Ross McPherson's recipe that appeared in *Alaska Magazine*.

Melt a cube of butter. Add a heaping cup of graham cracker crumbs. Mix them up and pat them down as crust in 9-inch round cake pans.

Place in layers in the order below.

1 6-ounce package of chocolate chips
1 6-ounce package of butterscotch chips
½ cup of coconut
½ can Eagle brand sweetened condensed milk
Again ½ cup coconut
And Again ½ can Eagle brand sweetened
condensed milk
Pat and top with 1 cup of pecans

Bake at 350 degrees for 35 minutes. Makes eight pieces. The total fat and calories per serving are 614 calories and 31.5 grams of fat each!

## Is there an organization for people who DON'T want to climb McKinley?

Yes, it's the *Mount McKinley (Non-Ascent) Club.*

Members have no intention of climbing McKinley, they meet each year at the base of the mountain and toast its spectacular beauty.

Pins are available to anybody but patches are given only to people who have actually been to a meeting. Notices are posted in Anchorage bars telling when and where the next meeting will occur.

*Pin from the Mount McKinley (Non-Ascent) Club.*

## Are there mountains in Alaska called VooDoo?

No, the correct name is the HooDoo Mountains.

## Everything in Alaska seems bigger, but even the clouds?

It's a fact. Noctilucent clouds are unique to sub-arctic latitudes in the northern and southern hemispheres and generally appear best during the six weeks following summer solstice. They are so large a single cloud can cover the entire state of Alaska (626,425 square miles!). Beat *that,* Texas!

Noctilucent clouds are pearl white waves of tiny ice crystals that coalesce in the upper limits of the atmosphere, approximately 50 miles above the earth. Traditional clouds form within seven miles of the ground making noctilucent clouds the highest forming clouds known.

## What was the biggest earthquake Alaska has ever experienced?

The Good Friday 1964 earthquake. It was the largest earthquake ever recorded in Alaska and at a 9.2 moment magnitude or Mw, it was the largest earthquake ever recorded in North America. It struck at 5:36 p.m. on March 27th and lasted a full four minutes, ending at 5:40 p.m. It rocked southcentral Alaska, Anchorage and Prince William Sound. The earthquake was so large it generated tsunamis (giant tidal waves) that went as far south as the northern coast of California. The Good Friday earthquake killed 131 people in Alaska.

### Isn't that half the population of Alaska?

No, smarty.

### How much damage did it cause?

Estimates varied, but Anchorage alone sustained more than $200,000,000 damage (in 1964 dollars) and 75 percent of the property was either destroyed or in need of major repairs.

*Damage caused in Anchorage at Turnagain Arms after Good Friday Earthquake in 1964. Photo courtesy National Oceanic and Atmospheric Administration, all rights reserved.*

### Is Alaska earthquake prone?

Sure is. Alaska averages 50,000 earthquakes a year. Fortunately most of them are small and in remote areas. Alaska has 11 percent of the world's earthquakes and 52 percent of all the earthquakes in the United States. Three of the six largest earthquakes recorded in the United States occurred in Alaska.

### Are there any large earthquakes predicted for the future?

Actually, yes. In the book *The Gulf of Alaska – Physical Environment and Biological Resources* which was compiled by the National Oceanic and Atmospheric Administration and the Department of the Interior, the authors documented the major earthquakes that occurred along the 4,000-kilometer plate boundary in the northern Pacific between Southeast Alaska and Kamchatka.

In 1971 the authors pointed out there were five "gaps" that would be likely sites for future large strain-relieving earthquakes. Since that prediction two moderately large earthquakes, a 7.6 Mw called the Sitka earthquake and a 7.5 Mw called the Saint Elias earthquake have occurred.

That leaves one gap close to civilization to worry about. It's the Yakataga seismic gap between the 1979 Saint Elias rupture in the east and the 1964 rupture zone of the Good Friday earthquake in the west. This area is believed to be capable of producing an 8.0 to 8.5 Mw earthquake within the next five years.

When the big one hits, remember you read about it here first. Perhaps earthquake insurance in Alaska isn't such a bad idea!

### Did Alaska have a wave that was more than 100 stories tall?

That's a big old scary *yes*. It happened on July 9, 1958 in Lituya Bay on the Alaska Panhandle. An 8.0 Mw earthquake shifted the opposite sides of the Fairweather fault. The jolt dislodged the side of a mountain that crashed into Lituya Bay that evening at 9:15 p.m. A wall of water came through the bay at the speed of 20 to 30 miles an hour, crashed onto land and rose to a height of 1,740 feet above the water line.

*Lituya Bay, Alaska. Photo courtesy National Aeronautics and Space Administration, all rights reserved.*

Three small boats were in the harbor at the time. One was washed over the spit guarding the entrance to Lituya Bay, one rode the wave out at anchor and the third was swept away, never to be seen again.

And it's happened before! Huge waves are believed to have occurred in the bay in 1853, 1874, 1899 and 1936. These were the largest waves ever to have been documented in *human history*.

### Does ice turn into fog?

Ice fog is a winter condition where the moisture in the air has turned into millions of tiny ice crystals. It occurs at temperatures below zero degrees Fahrenheit, usually along ocean and riverfronts. It is especially noticeable in Fairbanks from the combination of temperature inversions, auto and chimney emissions.

*Ice fog in North Pole, Alaska.*

### What is a sundog?

Suns that occasionally appear on either side of the sun during winter. The mirror images of the sun are caused by the reflection of sunlight off ice crystals in the air. This phenomenon sometimes results in the appearance of a halo around the sun or moon.

### During the winter, why do lights outdoors in Alaska seem to emit vertical light shafts instead of a halo?

Ice crystals. When the air temperature is between 5 and 15 degrees Fahrenheit, plate-like ice crystals tend to form in the air. The flat crystals orient with their flat sides, in the horizontal plane, as they tumble through the air, in the manner of falling leaves.

The vertical light columns are caused by reflection of light sources from the flat undersides of the falling crystals. These columns are seen above any bright light sources including streetlights and auto lights. Because the air temperature has to be so cold for them to appear, they are usually only observed in far northern locations.

### What is termination dust?

The first snow that falls from the sky and signals the end of Alaska's summer (but what a week it was!).

### How many ways can Eskimo's say the word snow?

If you said hundreds, you're wrong.

In 1911 Ralph Boas released a book called, *The Handbook of North American Indians*. In his book he mentioned that Eskimos have four distinct words for snow whereas English can say the same thing only through phrases (such as snow drift or falling snow).

In 1940 Benjamin Lee Whorf wrote an article titled, "Science and Linguistics" for *Technology Review* based on Boas work. In Whorf's article he increased the number of Eskimo words for snow, from four to seven, without any additional references to specific words. At the same time Whorf re-stated the misconception that English only had one word for snow without considering such words as slush, flurry or sleet.

Over the years the story became an urban legend. The number of words grew to ten, twenty, fifty and in 1984 a *New York Times* editorial claimed there were one hundred individual Eskimo words for snow! They were wrong.

### So how many are there?

First you must isolate which language (there are more than 20 Alaskan Native languages spoken throughout the state). Then count only word roots, not derivation words such as snowfall, snowflake or snowdrift.

Depending on which languages you choose you can come up with from two to twelve words. That's it. Not hundreds.

### Are there different types of snow?

Yup. Ten, according to the International Snow Classification for falling snow. You can see the complete chart on page 23.

### What is "breakup"?

Early spring in Alaska. That's when the frozen ground thaws into mucky swamp and the ice on the rivers begins to break apart. It's also the time when many relationships end, when people wake up to find that they have, indeed, been sleeping with a moose for the last six months.

### What is the significance of the Arctic Circle?

The Arctic Circle is usually depicted on maps at 66 degrees 33 minutes north latitude. South of this line the sun rises and sets daily. North of the line the sun remains above the horizon at midnight at midsummer and never rises during midwinter. If you are traveling on the Dalton Highway there is a wayside at mile 115 that was marked in 1992 by the Bureau of Land Management as the location where this invisible line crosses.

*Alaskan adventurer Judy Sohlstrom in front of the Arctic Circle sign.*

Unfortunately, it's wrong. It seems that planet earth has a slight wobble. Serbian climatologist Milutan

Milankovitch first pointed out that the tilt of Earth's axis shifts from about 22 to 24.5 degrees every 20,000 years. Then it shifts back over another 20,000 years. That wobble is called the Milankovitch Cycle.

### So how does that affect the Arctic Circle?

As the Earth's axis shifts 2.5 degrees every 41,000 years, that's 200 miles of movement. On a yearly basis it means a change of about 25 feet. So where the Arctic Circle was in 1992 isn't where it is today. But instead of moving the marker every year the Bureau of Land Management is simply going to wait until the circle moves back south again, in about 40,000 years.

### How did Turnagain Arm get its name?

After Captain James Cook finished exploring Prince William Sound he sailed west and found what looked to be a very promising inlet heading west-northwest. He sent men in smaller boats to keep exploring. As they went further into the inlet it became increasingly shallow, though the men were miles from any visible end to the water. Eventually only a small channel of water remained.

The channel curved and turned torturously forcing the boats to go not only side-to-side, but upstream and downstream to stay in deep enough waters. Upon their return and description of the winding waterway Captain Cook's cartographer marked the place "River Turnagain" because of all the twists and turns needed to navigate it. The Russians would call it "Vozvrashchenie" which means "Return Bay."

*Turnagain Arm.*

# International Snow Classification for falling snow.

| Type of Particle | Symbol | Example | Example | Graphic Symbol |
|---|---|---|---|---|
| Plate | F1 | | | |
| Stellar Crystal | F2 | | | |
| Column | F3 | | | |
| Needle | F4 | | | |
| Spatial Dendrite | F5 | | | |
| Capped Column | F6 | | | |
| Irregular Crystal | F7 | | | |
| Graupel | F8 | | | |
| Ice Pellet | F9 | | | |
| Hail | F0 | | | |

# Politics and War

### What is Alaska Day?

Every October 18th Alaskans celebrate the transfer of Alaska from Russian to United States ownership. The city of Sitka was the site of the transfer ceremonies and residents mark the day with parades, parties and period costumes.

### What branches of the United States Government were responsible for Alaska in the early years?

The United States Army was first (1867 – 1877), followed by the Treasury Department (1877 – 1879), then the United States Navy (1879 – 1884) and finally it became the District of Alaska in 1884 with an appointed territorial governor.

### Was Alaska really under the laws of the state of Oregon?

It was. The Organic Act of 1884 placed Alaskans under the state laws of Oregon. This rather unusual situation meant that any person accused of breaking a state law, who also insisted on a jury trial, would have to be shipped to Portland. Federal offenses however could be tried in Alaska.

### How did prostitutes help Alaska go from being a "district" to a "territory" and get a delegate in Congress?

It began in October of 1902, when Fred Rassmussen was arrested for running a whorehouse in Juneau, Alaska. The indictment was for "keeping a house of ill fame for the purpose of prostitution, fornication, and lewdness."

Fred could prove he wasn't on the property at the time but United States Attorney John J. Boyuce and Judge Melville Brown were on a moral crusade and were determined to make an example out of him. Fred hired attorney W. E. Crews to defend him.

Fred's trial was held December 9, 1902 and resulted in a hung jury. The prosecutors had trouble getting twelve more recruits to serve jury duty so they retried the case before a "petit jury" of six men, which federal law allowed in "unorganized territories." The attorney W.E. Crews objected stating that his client was an American citizen and deserved a full jury of his peers. Judge Brown wanted the case to proceed without delay and overruled Crews.

Fred Rassmussen was found guilty and given the maximum sentence – a year in jail, $2,500 bond and a lecture by Judge Brown.

Crews began appealing until it reached the United States Supreme Court. But he didn't appeal on the grounds Fred was innocent, but that although Alaska was unorganized, it was incorporated into the United States, and therefore its citizens did have full constitutional rights. Therefore, Fred Rassmussen was entitled to a trial by a twelve man jury.

Fred and Crews won, and in 1912 the "Rassmussen Decision" changed Alaska's official designation from "district" to "territory," setting in motion a measure giving it a delegate to Congress. Bob Bartlett became a token, non-voting congressional delegate in the United States Congress and Alaska convened a Territorial Legislature for representation within its own borders.

_Anchorage Daily Times_ proclaiming statehood. Photo used by permission, Alaska State Library - Historical Collections, all rights reserved.

### When did Alaska become a state?

On January 3, 1959, when President Eisenhower signed the statehood bill and the Alaska Territory became the 49th state of the United States.

**What did Senator Wesley Jones of Washington State do that put a burden on shipping in Alaska?**

He sponsored and helped pass the Merchant Marine Act of 1920 (also known as the Jones Act). This devious piece of legislation provided for the interchange of domestic or foreign carriers both on land and sea "except for Alaska." This meant that all shipping in and out of Alaska HAD to pass through Seattle, Washington before continuing to its final destination. Seattle profited handsomely while raising the cost of goods up to five times more than if shipped directly from other points in the Pacific. It wasn't until Alaska became a state in 1959 that the territorial restrictions were lifted.

**Did a man running to represent Alaska, in the United States House of Representatives, run on his record of reincarnation?**

Yes, in the 1994 campaign, Democrat Lawrence J. "Larry" Freiberger said he had lived in Alaska for three years, "but over 200 years counting past five incarnations." He lost the election.

**Does Alaska have four time zones?**

It did until October 30, 1983. At the state's request, the federal government reduced the time zones from four to two. The state is now predominately on Alaska time, or one hour earlier than Pacific time. The only residents of the state not on Alaska time are in the Aleutian Island communities of Atka, Adak, Shemya, Attu and on Saint Lawrence Island (which are on Aleutian-Hawaii time, one hour earlier than Alaska time).

**When did Alaska first come into prominence?**

During the period between 1897 and 1901, often referred to as the Gold Rush. Thousands of men and women flooded into Alaska, primarily headed toward the Klondike or Nome in search of gold. For more information on the Gold Rush see page 44.

**Does Alaska really pay people to retire in the state?**

Sort of. It's called the Longevity Bonus. It is a stipend paid to Alaskan residents over the age of 65 who have lived in the state for one year prior to January 1, 1997. Unfortunately if you're looking to retire in Alaska this program is no longer accepting new applicants.

The support amounts to $250 a month.

**Does Alaska pay other residents to live in the state?**

Yes. Alaska is the only state in the Union that pays its residents every year. Called the "Permanent Fund" it is a trust fund created by an amendment to the state constitution that sets aside a percentage of state oil and gas revenue for investment and protects it from government spending. Since 1982, Alaska residents have received an annual dividend of fund earnings. The first dividend was $1,000 for every eligible man, woman and child in the state.

**Are Alaskan pilots required to carry firearms as part of their emergency gear?**

They were until 2001. Pilots were required to carry firearms as a means of protection as well as for killing food. That law has been changed to leave it to the pilots discretion. Still required are one weeks food rations (down from two), fishing gear, an ax or hatchet and a mosquito headnet for each person on board. In the winter, snowshoes must be taken for each passenger.

*Aviator Duane Dahl and planes like this help transport Alaskans around some of the most rugged terrain in the world.*

**Why did the Federal Government issue a special coin, just for Alaskans living in the Matanuska Valley?**

It was because of a bookkeeping problem. There were 202 farm families who relocated to the

Matanuska Valley from the Midwest in the 1930s. These families (often referred to as colonists) bought goods on credit at the local Alaska Rural Rehabilitation Corporation (ARRC) commissary. Once the colonists farms began producing they were expected to pay back the ARRC commissary. Unfortunately, nobody kept track of the accumulating debt. This is in stark contrast to the modern system, where the accumulation of debt is closely monitored, but never addressed.

So, in February of 1936 the Federal Government issued between $3,000 and $3,500 worth of "bingles," a brand new coin, to each family to use at the ARRC commissary. Ideally the families would spend the bingles at the ARRC commissary and over time pay the government back. Everything looked good on paper, but problems started immediately.

To begin with, the term "bingle" is a nickname for poker chips, not a good connotation for money earned through hard work farming and land clearing.

Second, these independent farmers resented the fact that bingles could be used only to purchase goods from the ARRC commissary, creating a monopoly that barred them from comparative shopping.

*Bingles. A new coin for the Matanuska Valley. Photo courtesy Roy Brown of Roy's Coins in Anchorage, Alaska, all rights reserved.*

A "bingle black market" quickly formed when some farmers began using the coins to purchase drinks at the Matanuska Roadhouse and other taverns. The tavern owners then used the coins to purchase goods at the ARRC commissary.

In six months the bingle program was canceled. Today, collectors get hundreds of dollars for bingle coins.

**What governor tried to turn Alaska into an "agricultural state?"**

Jay Hammond, beginning his second term as governor in 1978. With hundreds of millions of dollars pouring into state coffers from North Slope oil Hammond decided to divert a little into creating an agricultural industry. Studies were conducted and the administration boldly predicted that the state would be self-sufficient in eggs and milk by 1990.

It would be a $100,000,000 bust. 84,000 acres in the Delta area, southeast of Fairbanks, was designated as Alaska's barley-producing capital. At the time, 70,000 of the acres were still covered in spruce forest.

The state of Alaska ordered $940,000 worth of railroad grain cars to carry Delta barley to the town of Seward where an $8,000,000 grain terminal was being built. Sensing a potential, the town of Valdez built a grain terminal in its harbor, costing $15,000,000 and financed by municipal bonds.

Alaskan politicians then set aside another 33,000 acres of heavily forested land on Point MacKenzie for dairy farming. A lottery was established and anyone who wanted to be a dairy farmer could apply, no experience necessary (which could serve as the Alaska State Motto). Winners would be given land, million-dollar lines of credit from the state and a set of instructions on how to establish a dairy farm.

In the meantime, Alaskans were growing increasingly affluent with the influx of oil money. It became very profitable for companies to ship in large quantities of fresh goods in refrigerated container ships.

It would be Sun Oil, an eastern oil company, not among the Prudhoe developers, that would ultimately destroy the Alaskan agricultural program.

Sun Oil had a new 790-foot container ship *The Great Land* that began servicing Alaska in 1976 delivering supplies to the pipeline. Sun Oil quickly switched it to hauling food in truck-trailers. By the early 1980s it was cheaper for Alaskans to buy milk shipped in from Seattle, over 2,000 miles away, than from their own local Matanuska Maid creamery.

First the dairy farms failed as their price to produce milk became higher than they could sell it for, then the barley farms failed without any dairy farmers to sell to.

The railroad grain cars that had been so proudly painted on the side with "Alaska Agriculture Servicing Alaska and the World" never delivered a grain of barley anywhere in Alaska, let alone anywhere else in the world. Construction on the grain terminal in Seward was halted in 1982 after being only half-built. The grain terminal in Valdez ended up costing the city $30,000,000 after interest costs were added in. Neither ever held a single grain of barley.

### Did Jay Hammond do anything else with the oil money?

He started the Alaska Renewable Resources Corporation (another ARRC) to provide venture capital to people who could "identify new products, markets, and technologies for renewable resource industries."

### How were loan applicants screened?

A Boston consultant was brought in and paid a fee of $38,000 to set up skill tests for potential entrepreneurs. He devised a three-stage test where applicants were judged on their ability to toss rings onto a pegboard on the floor, their precision stacking blocks (some of which had rounded edges), and their choices for selecting equipment that would help them survive in the wilderness. When the legislature found out about the "kiddie games" they were quietly abandoned.

### What kind of businesses did Jay Hammond's ARRC help fund?

$200,000 for a mushroom farm that couldn't turn a profit because the farmer delivered all the orders personally and socialized too much along the route.

$150,000 for a fox farm in North Pole where disease wiped out the entire breeding stock of two hundred.

$3,000,000 to a sawmill operator to build wood-fired powerhouses in Haines. It never produced one powerhouse before going bankrupt.

There was even a loan given to a man who invented a dog-powered washing machine!

The new Governor William Sheffield in 1982 eventually phased out the agency.

### Were atomic bombs used in Alaska?

Three times. By 1964 the nuclear devices were too large to be tested at the Nevada Test Site, so the Department of Defense and the Atomic Energy Commission chose Amchitka Island in Alaska. The first test was on an 80-kiloton explosion conducted in 1965 and was done to determine seismologists' ability to detect bombs other countries might be setting off underground.

The second detonation was called Milrow and took place October 2, 1969. Milrow was done to see how a larger explosion might damage the island, trigger seismic activity or generate tsunamis.

But the final explosion was the largest ever conducted in, on, or above, American soil. On November 6, 1971 a huge five-megaton bomb, designated Cannikin, was detonated and was 385 times more powerful than the bomb dropped on Hiroshima. It left a crater more than 1 mile wide and 40 feet deep. No additional tests were conducted but the final test helped spawn the formation of Greenpeace – the environmentalist group.

*Alaska could have been known as the "Radioactive State."*

### But wasn't there more involvement with atomic bombs?

Actually, there was. Through the 1950s and early 1960s the Atomic Energy Commission, along with scientist Edward Teller, were pushing for something called Project Chariot. The federal government wanted to create a deep-water harbor along the arctic coast, north of Kotzebue. But they wanted to do it by detonating up to six nuclear bombs!

Of course the harbor would have been locked in ice for nine months of the year, and in now-declassified documents Teller admitted he had no idea what the dynamics of the explosion would result in. The entire project was just another excuse to get more data about atomic detonations and had nothing to do with wanting a deep-water port. The plan was dropped as opposition began to mount.

**Did the government do anything else to Alaskans?**

Regrettably, yes. From 1955 to 1957 the United States Government conducted experiments with Alaskan Native men, women, and children. The Government gave oral doses of a low-level radioactive iodine to see whether the thyroid gland regulates the body's ability to withstand extreme cold. Fortunately, there didn't appear to be any harm caused by the testing but the participants weren't fully informed about the radioactive exposure. Most believed it was some sort of healthful treatment and only a few knew it had anything to do with medical experimentation. 30 years later the participants were paid approximately $67,000 each in a settlement between the North Slope Borough and the United States Government.

**Was Alaska prepared for World War II?**

Not at all. Alaska was a territory, and an ignored one at that. Nobody thought a military presence was really necessary. With the outbreak of World War II in Europe, September 1, 1939, America's two decades of isolationism gave way to considerations of self-defense.

Colonel Simon Bolivar Buckner, Jr. arrived in Anchorage July 22, 1940 to build a military command. He had to build one in a state with the highest mountains in North America, in thick forests, on tundra, permafrost and muskeg. The state had no good roads or reliable transportation systems, one short railroad and almost no electric power. There were no military defenses or communication systems.

The only military barracks housed four hundred soldiers armed with World War I rifles and the only piece of artillery was a single Russian cannon that served as a flower pot. Within two years Alaska would be the center of some of the most difficult battles of the war.

**Where did the Thousand Mile War take place?**

It was a World War II campaign in the Aleutian Islands to drive out the Japanese invaders. Alaska is the only state in the United States that was *occupied* by a foreign power during World War II. The islands of Attu and Kiska were occupied by the Japanese and the residents deported to prisoner of war camps. In a short time the occupation forces swelled to more than 14,000 troops.

**How long was the Thousand Mile War?**

About a thousand miles.

**Was there another name for the Thousand Mile War?**

It's also been called "The Forgotten War."

**What happened on the island of Attu?**

May 11, 1943 the United States landed 17,000 troops on Attu Island to take it back from the Japanese. Approximately 3,000 Japanese occupied the island and by May 29th the United States had suffered 550 deaths – but the Japanese had lost over 2,200. The remaining 800 Japanese soldiers staged a final charge and only 28 survived to be taken prisoner.

**How was Kiska retaken?**

July 28, 1943 approximately 5,000 Japanese soldiers evacuated the island of Kiska, undetected, under cover of fog. Nearly three weeks later 35,000 Allied troops invaded the deserted island and spent the next eight days searching for an enemy that had already left.

**How did an Eskimo's pee save an airplane?**

In 1942 Major Marvin "Muktuk" Marston was flying

entertainer Joe E. Brown to the Pribilofs to entertain the troops. On the flight out Marston's plane was forced down onto a frozen lake. Wind threatened to destroy the plane until local Eskimos drilled a hole in the ice, ran a line down from the plane and urinated in the hole to fill it. The urine froze fast around the line and anchored the plane.

## Can my pee save an airplane?

Good question. One never knows until one tries.

## How did phonograph records help Anchorage in the war effort during World War II?

A blackout was in effect. Cars drove with parking lights only and windows in homes were painted black with small slits for daylight. Unfortunately, there was a shortage of black paint. So residents improvised by dissolving phonograph records in acetone and used the result as a paint substitute.

## Did President Nixon and Emperor Hirohito of Japan really meet in Alaska?

The meeting took place on Elmendorf Air Force Base (Anchorage) in September 1971. It was the first time in the 2,500 year history of the Imperial Dynasty a ruling member had ever set foot on foreign soil.

## And Emperor Hirohito chose to go to Alaska?

Yeah. Go figure.

## Is land free in Alaska?

The Homestead Act became law on May 20, 1862. It was a program of public land grants to small farmers. Essentially the act provided that any adult citizen (or person who intended to become a citizen) could qualify for a grant of 160 acres of public land by paying a small registration fee and living on the land continuously for five years. If the settler was able to pay $1.25 per acre, he could obtain the land after only a six-month residence.

The act was extended to Alaska where a combination of poor soils, a short growing season and massive forests made the original intent of the law unworkable. Large tracts of Alaskan land were cleared unnecessarily as homesteaders tried to fulfill the conditions of the law. Although the land was free, homesteading took a lot of money. Only the lucky ones who homesteaded land around Alaska's few cities ever found their land had any value. Homesteading ended in 1974.

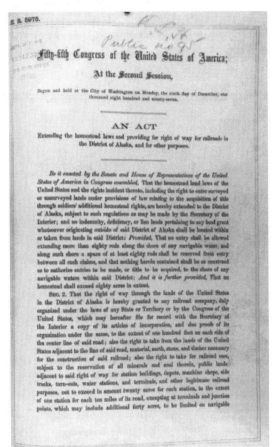

*Extension of the Homestead Act to Alaska. Photo courtesy of the United States National Archives and Records Administration (NARA), all rights reserved.*

## Do Alaskans take wilderness guiding seriously?

Very! According to Alaskan Statutes: Sec. 08.64.360 the penalty for practicing medicine without a license is a class A misdemeanor. But it is a federal offense to lead tours in a National Park without a license.

## What license do I need to drive a snowmachine in Alaska?

As of the year 2002, none.

There is no state helmet law, no required operator training, no minimum age requirement, no state speed limits and no formal trail system. All you need is a snowmachine and a tank full of gas. Actually, it doesn't even need to be full.

*Technically there is one place where helmets and a drivers license are required. That's on Bureau of Land Management (BLM) land. However, the law is rarely enforced and tickets have been overturned in court.*

*This is a photo of anybody driving a snowmachine in Alaska. Photo courtesy Peter Van Dyne, all rights reserved.*

# Cities and Towns

**What Alaska city is described as being "only a half-hour from Alaska"?**

That would be Anchorage, with about half of the state's population. Anchorage began life in 1915 as a tent city during the construction of the Alaska Railroad and was incorporated in 1920. It was centrally planned, neat and orderly in a state that is anything but. Today it is the hub of the state's economic activity. Much of the livelihood of the city's more than 200,000 residents come from federal, state or municipal government jobs, oil, or one of the service industries.

*Anchorage skyline.*

**What did anthropologist Dr. Richard Leakey say while lecturing in Anchorage in 1994?**

*"It's considered fact that all human habitation of the United States. North America, and South America started right here – all early inhabitants came over the land bridge from Asia and probably came right through here.*

*And considering what I saw this morning as I looked out of my [Anchorage] hotel room. I can't understand why they didn't turn right around and go back where they came from."*

**How did Anchorage get its name?**

From the United States Post Office. In April 1915 when preparations were made for establishing a post office, all mail was sent to "Anchorage." Maps and news accounts quickly adopted the name. Then in August 1915 residents were given the opportunity to decide the name of their town. Suggested names included Matanuska, Alaska City, Ship Creek, Winalaska, Gateway and Lane. In the end the residents cast their vote for Alaska City. However, the federal government concluded that a change would be unwarranted. Despite petitions by the Chamber of Commerce, Anchorage it has remained.

**It sounds like the Federal Government always had a strong grip on Anchorage. How did Anchorage residents ever get free from it?**

It all started because prostitutes were not allowed to bid on land in the new town site of Anchorage. They squatted first at the mouth (oh, there's a lovely image) of Ship's Creek, then on both sides of a dead-end thoroughfare near Ninth and C Streets. People into punishment went up Ship's Creek for a paddling.

The town site was controlled by a board made up of Lieutenant Fred Mears of the Alaska Engineering Commission, A. Christensen of the United States General Land Office and T. M. Hunt, Supervisor of the United States Forest Service. The board argued fiercely about how to dispose of the prostitutes. Hunt was determined not to allow prostitutes to occupy national forest lands. However, A. Christensen quietly had the Marshal move them over the city border and into the forest during the night.

When Hunt found out he was outraged. Now the law forced him to issue "camping permits" to each of the women! After some negotiations Hunt convinced the Anchorage city planners to offer a free camping area in the town and the prostitutes moved back.

Unfortunately, Hunt discovered the Forest Service was still responsible for them under its administrative rules. What was worse, they seemed to be settling down permanently. On January 6, 1917 Assistant District Forester Charles Flory wrote a "Strictly Confidential" letter to the District Forester recommending the Forest Service relinquish all administrative power over the town site of Anchorage. The embarrassment of running a red light district proved too much for the bureaucrats in Washington D.C. and they gave up their seat on the town's governing board.

Anchorage's city fathers had the prostitutes to thank for their freedom from federal interference in city affairs.

**I've heard that Anchorage occasionally has extremely strong winds. Is that true?**

Unfortunately, yes. Gusts to 80 miles an hour do occur on a fairly regular basis and in the winter of 1980 winds were clocked at 140 miles per hour! That's twice hurricane force. The state of Alaska ended up building a 10 foot-high fence for the purpose of keeping trailers from blowing across the road during windstorms and distracting drivers.

**Is there really a staircase made out of solid jade?**

Sure is. It's in the Anchorage Sheraton, built by the Calista Native Corporation in the early 1980s. The hotel's designer ordered a $700,000 solid jade staircase as the centerpiece of the lobby.

*The solid jade staircase in the Anchorage Sheraton.*

**Is there a chocolate waterfall in Anchorage?**

Yes! At Alaska Wild Berry Products you can see the largest chocolate "waterfall" ever built. Conceived by Peter Eden and designed by Homer artist Mike Sirl, it was built in 1994. In 1996 Sampson Steel Company modified it.

For the chocoholic it holds an amazing 3,400 pounds of real liquid chocolate that cascades down a 20 foot chocolatefall. (No diving please.)

*Close-up of the solid jade staircase in the Anchorage Sheraton.*

Unfortunately, jade was too slippery to walk on and it had to be covered with carpeting. Today exposed strips along each side give a small peak at the wealth lying directly underneath your feet.

*The 20 foot high chocolatefall at Alaska Wild Berry Products in Anchorage.*

**What is that strange building that looks like an igloo between Denali Park and Anchorage?**

It's the only hotel in Alaska that doesn't allow loitering. Leon Smith and his wife Elizabeth started building "The Igloo" in 1972 as a 40-unit hotel. Although supposedly built to code, the hotel has never actually opened for business. As of early 2002 it stands empty, waiting to be completed at mile marker 188.5 of the Parks Highway. There is however a snack shop, fuel and postcards for sale on the site.

*The Igloo on the Parks Highway.*

**How was Fairbanks founded?**

Because of a chance meeting between trader E.T. Barnette, prospector Felix Pedro and a river that was too shallow.

It all began when Captain E.T. Barnette found himself stranded at Saint Michael in July 1901 with 125 tons of trade goods on hand. He had planned to take the load on his boat, the *Arctic Boy*, to the Valdez-Eagle crossing, approximately 400 miles up the Tanana River, above Fort Weare, where he wanted to establish a trading post. Unfortunately, his boat, the *Arctic Boy*, had just wrecked on the rocks in Saint Michael Harbor.

So Barnette persuaded Captain C.W. Adams to lease his boat, the *Lavelle Young,* to complete the journey.

The *Lavelle Young* reached the mouth of the Chena River, turned in and traveled seven more miles before the Chena River branched into several channels, all of them too shallow for the *Lavelle Young's* four-foot draft. Captain Adams decided it was impossible to go any farther. He called Barnette to the pilot house and told him he had "guaranteed

to take you as far as the boat would go up the Tanana. I can't cross mountains with it."

Captain Adams then made one last attempt to get through the Chena River and back to the Tanana River. Adams ran out of water. Barnette was forced to unload on a high timbered bank.

At about this time, up in the hills, Felix Pedro and his partner Tom Gilmore were about to return to Circle for supplies when they spotted smoke on the horizon. Standing on a hill overlooking the valley they watched the steamboat *Lavelle Young* dock along the bank. It took the men three days to get to the Chena River where they had seen the steamboat. Pedro and Gilmore stocked up on beans, flour and bacon. They also showed the crew some gold samples they had taken from a nearby stream.

This meeting between Felix Pedro and E.T. Barnette, on that fall day in 1901, established the location of the future town of Fairbanks on the Chena River.

*Felix Pedro.. Photo used by permission, Alaska State Library - Historical Collections, all rights reserved.*

**So why is it called "Fairbanks"?**

Because of a deal made between E.T. Barnette and federal Judge James Wickersham at Saint Michael. Wickersham would help Barnette succeed in his ventures if Barnette would name his post "Fairbanks" in honor of Republican Senator Charles

W. Fairbanks of Indiana. Barnett also donated land for a courthouse and jail.

## Why is the Old Federal Building responsible for Fairbanks becoming the largest city in interior Alaska?

Fairbanks and Chena City were in competition to become the primary supply center for interior Alaska. Chena had the advantage with a better location for steamboat traffic. So in 1904 E.T. Barnette (Fairbanks founder) donated land for the first courthouse and federal jail. The first building burned down in 1906. The second building settled badly, had insufficient bearing walls and badly ventilated washrooms. Two fires further damaged the structure. Finally the Treasury Department commissioned architect George N. Ray of Washington, D.C. to design the new Federal Building for Fairbanks.

With its dedication on August 13, 1934 the Federal Building put Fairbanks firmly ahead of Chena. Fairbanks had the government offices and Chena did not. Today, Fairbanks is a bustling city of 35,000 people while the city of Chena is gone.

*The Old Federal Building in Fairbanks.*

The Old Federal Building is representative both of Art Deco design influences and construction materials popular in the 1930s. Gravel used for the project was hand-shoveled out of the Chena River and trucked over to the site. There is even a copper roof above the courtroom.

## Weather-wise, what's Fairbanks claim to fame?

Fairbanks has the most rigorous climate of any city in the United States. The minimum temperature recorded is –66 degrees Fahrenheit and the maximum is 99 degrees Fahrenheit. That's a difference of 165 degrees! It gets worse. The average number of days with freezing temperatures is 233, and freezing temperatures have been recorded *every month of the year* except July! Fairbanks residents believe that the weather "eliminates the riff-raff."

## Is it true that bacon saved the town of Fairbanks?

Yes. In April of 1906 a three-story building on the corner of First Street and Cushman Avenue caught fire and burned rapidly. A cupola on top of the building fell and broke the fire hydrant on the corner. This seemingly insignificant event caused the water to escape from the fire hydrant and the pressure in all other hydrants dropped.

There was little water to use against the fire so Volney Richmond, manager of the Northern Commercial Company store, ordered the bacon in the warehouse to be used as fuel in the power plant. With the bacon burning the water pressure for the fire hoses was maintained. More of the town would have burned if the bacon hadn't saved the day. Try **that** with grits!

## Did Fairbanks license prostitutes in 1905?

Sort of. Fairbanks was a well-organized city and it was guided by Judge Wickersham's policy of taxing vice for civic betterment. In 1905, the city attorney would greet women arriving in the city with the question, "Are you a lady or a whore? If you are a lady, pass on, if you are a whore, seventeen dollars and a half." Apparently this is the sort of questioning one can get away with in Alaska. According to an informant for the *Valdez News* the take averaged $1,200 a month!

## Is it true that outhouses are now illegal in Fairbanks?

Actually – not yet. In 2001 the Fairbanks North Star Borough Assembly passed an ordinance that required people who live near sewer and water lines to hook up or dig a septic system. So this means NEW outhouses may not be erected…and the old ones must be removed…within 10 years. One of the assembly members, Jim Holm, was quoted as saying, "As a society, we can make rules that inhibit activities of other people, and if they don't like it, they can move farther out into the woods."

**Is there really a roadhouse outside Fairbanks called "Skinny Dick's"?**

Yup. The full name is "Skinny Dick's Halfway Inn."

*Skinny Dick's Halfway Inn.*

**Where's the town of Coldfoot?**

Sixty miles north of the Arctic Circle on the Dalton Highway. It's the northernmost truck stop in the United States. Coldfoot was originally called Slate Creek, but the name was changed around 1900 after a gold strike on the Koyukuk River brought prospectors in. The gold stampeders made it all the way to Slate Creek before the harsh interior weather gave them "cold feet" and forced them to turn back. It's been known as Coldfoot ever since.

**Was the town of Deadhorse named after a dead animal?**

Nope. Deadhorse is a support location for the nearby Prudhoe Bay oil field. It received its name from the Deadhorse airport, which was named after the construction company that built the airport, which was named after a dead animal.

**How big is the town of Olnes?**

Originally established in 1904-1905 it once had more than 200 people living there, two roadhouses, three stores, three saloons and nine mining operations. By the year 2000 the population was one.

**Is the North Pole in Alaska?**

The place on the globe known as the North Pole is not, but there is a town in Alaska called North Pole. About 20 minutes from Fairbanks, North Pole got its name in the early 1950s as a gimmick to lure toy manufacturers to town. The toy companies never came but the holiday spirit is alive and well, year round, in a town with candy cane street lamps and a 42 foot high fiberglass statue of Santa Claus that weighs about 900 pounds and has a 33 foot waist!

*Santa Claus statue at the Santa Claus House in North Pole.*

**If you send a letter to Santa does it go to the North Pole?**

Actually thousands do, and the North Pole Post Office opens them all. If the letter is from a child they receive a response from a volunteer (one of Santa's helpers) saying they hope everything the child wants will be under the tree. If it's from an adult requesting assistance, the Post Office sends it back to the originating city where it is turned over to a social service agency to help.

**What if I want to get a letter from Santa?**

Write to:

Santa Claus
325 S. Santa Claus Lane
North Pole, AK 99705-9998

To receive a handwritten response the letters must arrive by December 1st, form letters will be used for any letters received by December 5th.

## And if I just want to get my letters postmarked from the North Pole?

Stamp and address each item you wish to have postmarked. Then put all the items into a larger envelope or box and include a note requesting the North Pole postmark. Send those to:

North Pole Cancellations
U.S. Postal Service
5400 Mail Trail
Fairbanks, AK 99709-9996

For delivery by Christmas these must arrive by December 10th.

*The North Pole Post Office in North Pole, Alaska.*

### What is the North Pole Monument?

A red-and-white pole proudly displayed in the town of North Pole. On December 11, 1951 an Alaska Airlines DC-4 flew from Fairbanks to the geographic North Pole so the crew could drop a nine-foot-long pole, painted like a candy cane on the top of the world. It was a publicity stunt to "properly mark the top of the earth."

It all began as an idea of Stan Garson who wanted to place a pole at the Pole. He wanted it to look like the picture in children's books. As part of the project, 4,800 letters were written to Santa Claus from children from all over the United States. Volunteers answered the letters which were to be dropped with the pole.

The pole was taken on a grand tour from New York to Los Angeles for television appearances. Finally, the pole returned to Fairbanks accompanied by actress Carolina Cotton, the world champion female yodeler. A gala reception was held and the pole and letters were flown out and dropped from 7,000 feet

above the geographic North Pole. Then things start to get a little murky.

According to the plaque the pole was dropped at the magnetic North Pole (which is in northern Canada), and "later recovered by the city of North Pole." Not exactly. The news accounts of 1951 stated it was dropped on the *geographic* North Pole (in the Arctic Ocean) and since the pole was dropped from a plane at 7,000 feet it would have plunged through the ice deep into the ocean. There's no way that pole would have ever been recovered.

*The North Pole...Pole, in North Pole, Alaska.*

What actually happened is there were TWO poles made by the N.C. Machine shop. The first one was deemed too heavy for the flight and a second, lighter one was made. The lighter pole was the one dropped and the heavier one ended up in the junkyard. In 1972 the junkyard was being cleared of old automobiles and the heavier pole was "rediscovered." The North Pole Jaycees cleaned it up and on July 4th, 1976, proudly erected the "recovered" pole.

### What is the most powerful thing in North Pole?

KJNP radio station. KJNP stands for King Jesus North Pole, the most powerful radio station in all Alaska. Would you expect anything less from a station that advertises itself as the "Voice of God"?

KJNP radio station also has one other unique feature; it's housed in the largest sod-roofed log cabin in the state and is surrounded by a community of sod-roofed cabins called "Jesus Town." And yes, they do offer tours.

*One of the sod-roofed log cabins in "Jesus Town," KJNP radio.*

### When was the city of Nome founded?

Nome sprang up practically overnight when word leaked in 1898 of the discovery of gold on Anvil Creek by the Three Lucky Swedes. (Actually one of them, Lindeberg, was a Norwegian but we digress.) By the next summer there were 10,000 people in the area. There were 20,000 people the following year when gold was discovered in the beach sands. Suddenly Nome was the largest city in Alaska. Today it is a community of about 3,000 people.

*The "Three Lucky Swedes." From left to right, John Brynteson, Jafet Lindeberg and Erik Lindblom. Photo used by permission, Alaska State Library - Historical Collections, all rights reserved.*

### Who discovered gold in the beach sand of Nome?

An old feeble prospector who was too sick to go to the creeks and toil in the permafrost. John Hummell decided to walk to the beach and pan some of the black sand. Much to his amazement gold appeared in his pan. Within hours men and women were on the beach turning over sand hoping to strike it rich. That first summer of 1899, 2,000 miners, along a 42-mile stretch of beach, took out $2,000,000 of gold. This was the only place in Alaska where gold was so easily accessible.

Tex Rickard was one of Nome's more famous residents. He made a fortune in Nome and turned it into a profitable investment in New York City called Madison Square Garden. Wyatt Earp also lived in Nome for a while and was part owner of the Dexter Saloon.

*Prospecting for Gold on the beach of Nome. Photo used by permission, Alaska State Library - Historical Collections, all rights reserved.*

### How did Nome get its name?

According to one story it was a mistake by a British mapmaker in 1853. He misread the notation that said "Name?" for a nearby cape and called it Cape Nome.

### What does it say on the city seal for Nome?

"Auro-Sub Nive-Ditesco" which according to Nome city ordinance number 0-94-6-1 means, "I dig for gold beneath the snow."

### Why was Nome called a "One Horse Town"?

Because it was! In 1952 Prince was the last remaining horse in the town of Nome. Prince's owner Herman

Hoop decided to turn him into dog food because he was unable to get enough food for the horse to make it through the winter. Prince became a national celebrity when a campaign was mounted to "Save Prince." Money and food were secured and Prince was saved, as the last horse of a "One Horse Town."

**What was once one of the signs of spring in Nome?**

The green rivulets of shark repellent running down the street. Honest! In World War II lend-lease aircraft and other military planes carried a nontoxic dye in case of an "un-scheduled water landing" (crash) in the Pacific Ocean. The dye would mark the crash site and as a bonus contained shark repellent to protect any potential survivors.

Dye was stored in a shack on Steadman Street. When water from the spring snow melt got high enough, dye flowed over the curb and ran into storm drains along the street.

It's obviously a very good shark repellent since Nome has never reported a single shark attack.

**What brings atheists to the Holy Rosary Catholic Church in Dillingham?**

The water! The well water from the Catholic Church is pure and clean, people have been taking it home for more than 40 years. A city well, only a short distance away, provides water but it is brown and frequently undrinkable.

During a drought, when other wells around town were drying up, the well at the Catholic Church continued to pour forth. Holy water, indeed.

*Father Jim Kelly of the Holy Rosary Parish filling up a jug from the Catholic Church's well water. Photo courtesy of Father Kelly.*

The late Father Jim Kelley said all are welcome to the water for free, but donations are accepted from those who are able.

**Is the Holy Rosary Catholic church known for anything else?**

It's the longest parish in the United States. Stretching more than 1,971.6 miles (the distance from Boston to Denver), The Father ministers to several hundred parishioners, "and 19 active volcanoes" across the frontiers of Alaska. He does this by flying into remote villages in small planes.

**What city has the longest days and nights?**

That would be Barrow. During summer months the sun doesn't set from around mid-May until August. In winter the longest night is 67 days long (approximately 1,608 hours).

**What else is Barrow known for?**

It is the seat of the North Slope Borough which taxes all the Prudhoe Bay oil field. In 1999 Barrow was the richest city per capita in the United States and possibly the world.

**What did Barrow do with its new wealth?**

An Inupiaq whaling captain Eben Hopson was elected the first mayor of Barrow in 1972. He pledged that his constituents would have all the amenities of people in Fairbanks and Anchorage and authorized the construction of the Barrow Utilidor, a sewer and water system that would be installed in heated tunnels burrowed beneath the permafrost. Debt swelled to more than 1.2 billion dollars as public works projects were undertaken, and this for a city of less than six thousand people!

At one time Barrow's capital budget was $300 million per year or $50,000 per resident! More than the city of Chicago spent for three million residents.

**What ends in Valdez?**

The Trans-Alaska Pipeline. Valdez is a small coastal city of about 3,000 people in southcentral Alaska on the northern shore of Prince William Sound. The city was originally established during the gold rush but the original location was destroyed by a tsunami from the Good Friday earthquake.

The town's name is a legacy of Spanish explorations in Alaskan waters in the 18th century. Incidentally, Alaskans do not use the Spanish pronunciation of Val-*dez* but rather Val-d*eez*. Anyone calling it Val-*dez* is quickly labeled an outsider.

### Who founded the city of Juneau?

Joe Juneau. He was a prospector in southeast Alaska who discovered gold in 1880. Joe's discovery led to the city's founding and development. Juneau's gold is one of the largest lodes of quartz gold in the world.

Juneau (the city) became the official capital of Alaska in 1906. In 1974 Alaskans voted to move the capital to a site between Fairbanks and Anchorage. They chose the city of Willow in 1976 but the whole idea was dropped when Alaskans rejected funding the move in 1982. Juneau is the only state capital in the continental United States that is inaccessible by road.

*Joe Juneau. Photo used by permission, Alaska State Library - Historical Collections, all rights reserved.*

### What is the story behind Juneau's "Glory Hole"?

The Alaska-Treadwell Gold Mining Company was the first large-scale mining operation in Alaska. During its 35 years of operation the Treadwell mine produced gold worth almost $72,000,000. Its stamp mills (the machinery that extracted gold particles from ore brought up) were the largest in the world.

People called the Treadwell mine the "Glory Hole" because so many of the workers plunged to their deaths (were sent to their glory) down the more than 2,000 foot-deep mineshaft. The reputation, only slightly exaggerated, was that the Glory Hole averaged one accidental death every day.

*Juneau - Capital of Alaska.*

### Was Juneau always the capital of Alaska?

No, the original capital was the town of Kodiak. It has had several ups and downs including being buried in 18 inches of ash after the Katmai volcano eruption in 1912 and was partially destroyed by a tsunami following the Good Friday earthquake of 1964. Today it has become one of Alaska's premier fishing ports.

The next capital was the town of Sitka, a community today of about 8,000 people on Baranof Island in southeast Alaska. It was originally a Tlingit village, but when the Russians retaliated for the destruction of their Fort Saint Michael in 1802 they drove the

Indians off and appropriated the site. During the Russian occupation it was called New Archangel.

Sitka may be small in population but it's big on size. Sitka is approximately 4,719 square miles making it the largest city in North America. The entire state of Rhode Island is only 1,214 square miles.

Juneau wouldn't become the capital of the Alaska Territory until 1900.

**What was Creek Street in the town of Ketchikan known for?**

It was a bustling red light district that served the fishing fleets. Built on pilings edging Ketchikan Creek it was "the only place in the world where both the fish and fishermen go upstream to spawn."

*Main street of Ketchikan around 1900. Photo used by permission, Alaska State Library - Historical Collections, all rights reserved.*

**Why did a prostitute named "Black Mary" win the undying gratitude of the residents of Saint Petersburg?**

Well, not because of her vocational aptitudes or abilities (as far as we know). She saved the town from burning. During a large blaze the firemen discovered that the local stream was too low for pumping. Mary, described as being a "mountain of a woman," took off her clothes and sat in the creek damning it up. The firefighters were then able to pump the water and put out the fire.

**What town is known as "The Halibut Fishing Capital of the World"?**

Homer, Alaska. It's located on the southwestern edge of the Kenai Peninsula on Kachemak Bay near the mouth of the Cook Inlet.

*Stuart Varner and Jim Stuhr with halibut catch.*

**Where was the starting point for people entering Alaska during the Klondike Gold Rush?**

Skagway, a boomtown that sprang up at the head of the Lynn Canal in southeast Alaska in 1897.

**Was a man's head really on display in the town of Skagway?**

Gruesome, but true. It all started one night on September 15, 1902 when an unknown man decided to withdraw some money from the Skagway Branch of the Canadian Bank of Commerce. The problem was the unknown man didn't have an account at the bank, so he took along a gun in his right hand and dynamite in the left and went to rob the place.

*Skagway, Alaska circa 1900. Photo used by permission, Alaska State Library - Historical Collections, all rights reserved.*

During the holdup the robber was startled when a customer named John Price entered the bank unexpectedly to make a deposit. The robber fired his gun. The shot set off the unstable dynamite leaving the bank in shambles and the would-be-robber in critical condition. Fortunately, everyone else was fine. A few hours later the robber died at the railroad hospital.

The banker hosed down the bank with the help of the military, dug up the street outside and hauled it all down to the Skagway River. He then ran everything through sluice boxes and recovered more gold dust than was believed on hand in the bank at the time of the blast. Not a single dollar was lost.

Nobody in town knew who the attempted robber was, so his remains were eventually placed in a sack and thrown into a woodshed after being studied at a medical clinic. (We're not making this up folks!)

Three men, including W.T. White, later discovered the body. The skeleton was cremated but White kept the skull. White then presented the skull to Dr. L.S. Keller in 1910, who later gave it to Martin Itjen. Mr. Itjen proudly displayed it in his museum until 1926, when the museum was closed.

In 1926 the head was finally buried. The inscription on his tombstone read:

*The nob of the man is all that is here.*
*Will look for the rest when we get over there.*

### How did the town of Chicken get its name?

Because nobody that lived there was a very good speller. Legend has it the residents wanted to name it ptarmigan, a grouse-like bird that is the state bird of Alaska. Unfortunately, nobody knew how to spell ptarmigan, so they named their town after a ptarmigan look alike – the chicken.

*On the left - a chicken. On the right - a ptarmigan.*

### What town is referred to in the book titled *The Strangest Town in Alaska*?

The most unusual town of Whittier. Created by the United States Government during World War II as a port and petroleum delivery center. Some of the stranger facts about Whittier…

* For the first 50 years of Whittier's existence it was accessible only by boat or train. No cars could drive there until the year 2000.

* The road to Whittier isn't very long - only 12 miles from Portage Glacier. But it was one of the most expensive in Alaska. It's a toll road (the first ever in Alaska) that cost $80 million to build. Cars, trucks, buses and trains all share a 2.6 mile long alternating-direction, one-lane, shared-use tunnel.

* The first electrical line to Whittier was essentially a giant extension cord. A military bomber flew out of Anchorage with a spool of electrical wiring in the bomb bay, and a weight tied to one end. The line was played out, lying over the top of 3,500-foot Mt. Maynard, the end finally dropping into Whittier. The lines were connected and Whittier was electrified. (Wait until the guy at the source gets his electric bill!)

* The entire city of Whittier was mothballed as surplus in September of 1960 when Major General J.H. Michaels made a brief announcement in Anchorage that Whittier was to be "inactivated." Approximately 800 people lived in Whittier in 1960 when the announcement was made and of those 800, a skeletal maintenance crew of 48 was to remain.

* Finally, if you plan on visiting Whittier, bring rain gear. Annual precipitation figures average 174 inches (14.8 feet!) and annual snowfall is around 260 inches (almost 22 feet).

### What is so unusual about the buildings in Whittier?

The town once had two of the largest buildings in Alaska that together were designed to house 30,000 people.

The Buckner Building resembles a land-based aircraft carrier. Almost as big as a battleship, the

Buckner Building was created as a self-sufficient, "city under one roof." With approximately 273,660 square feet of space it had a rifle range, bowling alley, movie theater and a radio station. The United States Army built the Buckner at a cost of $6,000,000 (in the 1950s!). The Buckner Building is connected by an underground tunnel to another huge structure known as the "Hodge."

*The Buckner Building in Whittier.*

Ninety percent of the population of Whittier (less than 300 people in the year 2000) live in the "Hodge," (now known as the Begich Tower or BTI). Finished in 1956 it rose 14 stories above the shore and when completed was the tallest building in Alaska.

At its height Whittier only had 1,200 residents (mostly military).

*The Begich Tower in Whittier.*

### What happened to the town of Kennicott?

It all began with two prospectors in 1900. Jack Smith and Clarence Warner spotted a large green spot on the mountain between the Kennicott Glacier and McCarthy Creek. That green spot turned out to be one of the richest deposits of copper ore ever found anywhere in the world.

In 1906 the Kennecott Mines Company (later incorporated in 1915 as Kennecott Copper Corporation) was formed. The mining company was supposed to take the name of the nearby Kennicott glacier but was misspelled. To this day the town and glacier are spelled Kennicott but the mines and company are spelled Kennecott.

The town of Kennicott had the copper, but the problem was in the transportation. So, in the spring of 1908 construction began on the CR&NW or Copper River Northwestern Railway. The line ran 196 miles from the town of Kennicott to Cordova where the Alaska Steamship Company could take the copper ore to Tacoma, Washington. During construction there was so little faith in the CR&NW that it was nicknamed the "Can't Run and Never Will." In the end it did run and transported more than 200 million dollars worth of copper ore.

All the mines under Kennicott were connected by tunnels. The combined underground workings are several hundred miles in total length and go down more than 2,800 feet!

Copper kept the town busy and prosperous with 500 to 600 residents. The downfall came with the falling prices of copper. Prices dropped so low that finally, in 1938, the mines were closed and train service was discontinued. November of 1938 saw the last train leave Kennicott for Cordova taking most of the remaining people with it.

That would have been the end except for an amazing act. In 1941 the Kennecott Copper Corporation voluntarily gave the CR&NW right-of-way to the federal government for the construction of a public highway. Today a handful of people live in Kennicott, providing mostly tourist related services, and they are surrounded by the Wrangell-St. Elias National Park and Preserve established in 1980.

### Who was the Kennicott Glacier named after?

Robert Kennicott in 1899. Robert was the director of the Western Union Telegraph Expedition in 1865 and 1866 when the company was exploring an overland telegraph route across Alaska to Siberia. (For more about the Western Union Telegraph Expedition see page 54.)

**What did Wyatt Earp, the famed Arizona gunman call the town of Wrangell?**

"Absolutely Fabulous."

Not really. Earp actually called it "Hell on wheels." His wife Josie sized it up as another Tombstone. The United States Marshal for Alaska offered Mr. Earp the job of deputy, but Earp turned it down. He did fill in for a few days until another gunman could be found.

**What does a fat Alaskan that died in 1918, a Swedish born pathologist named Johan Hultin and the town of Brevig Mission, Alaska have in common that could save millions of lives someday?**

The influenza virus. In 1918 and 1919 the world was hit with one of the most devastating plagues ever experienced by humankind. It is estimated that over those two years between 20 and 40 million people died worldwide from influenza.

Beginning with a mild case of runny nose, it would quickly turn into a flu or pneumonia. Death could result in as short a time as 48 hours. Mass graves were dug to dispose of the bodies before more people could be infected.

Unfortunately, the virus was never identified, so if it ever re-emerges doctors may not have time to develop a vaccine.

That's where Dr. Johan Hultin comes in. Studying viruses since 1949 Dr. Hultin heard a colleague say that, "perhaps if someone went north, they'd be able to find frozen bodies – and an intact virus." So, in 1951 Dr. Hultin went north to the village of Brevig Mission hunting for bodies and the virus. He found the bodies but the technology of the day didn't allow him to identify the virus.

Lucky for us Dr. Hultin was patient. He returned to Brevig Mission in 1997 and with the permission of the village council once again began digging, looking for influenza victims. That's when "Lucy" was unearthed.

Named after the Latin word "lux" for light, Lucy had outlasted all the other bodies because of a two-inch layer of fat that helped preserve her organs. Her lungs were removed, sent to Washington, D.C. and a vaccine is being developed.

So, if the deadly influenza virus ever does strike again, and you have the vaccine, you'll be able to thank an obese Alaskan, a Swedish born pathologist and the town of Brevig Mission, Alaska.

*Dr. Hultin (in center of photo) during his original Alaskan dig in 1951. Photo used by permission of Johan Hultin, M.D., all rights reserved.*

**How many people live in the entire state?**

619,500 as of the 1999 United States Census Bureau estimates. That makes Alaska the third least populous state (behind Wyoming and Vermont). *Because of its size* Alaska is the least populated state averaging 1.05 square miles per person. Wyoming is next with .20 square miles per person.

**Where is the mysterious "Silent City"?**

On June 21, 1888 Richard Willoughby took a picture of a city that appeared to be suspended in front of the Fairweather Range at the head of the Glacier Bay ice field.

The picture was actually an over-exposed image of the town Bristol, England. Richard (who liked to call himself "professor") peddled hundreds of photographs from the glass plate negative and it would be the hoax he would always be remembered for. Ironically other photographers or studios then later attempted to photograph The Silent City, but obviously...with no success.

# Gold!

**What triggered the stampede of people into Alaska in 1898?**

A headline and story in the *Seattle Post-Intelligencer* newspaper. The headline read,

### GOLD! GOLD! GOLD! GOLD!

...followed by another stampede out of Alaska a few months later:

### COLD! COLD! COLD! COLD!

Just kidding. This is what they said in the article:

**"ON BOARD THE STEAMSHIP PORTLAND, 3AM** – At 3 o'clock this morning the Steamship *Portland* from St. Michael's for Seattle, passed up sound with more than a ton of solid gold on board and 68 passengers. In the captain's cabin are three chests and a large safe filled with the precious nuggets. The metal is worth nearly $700,000 and the most of it was taken out of the ground in less than three months of last winter. In size the nuggets range from the size of a pea to a guinea egg. Of the 68 miners on board, hardly a man has less than $7,000 and one or two have more than $100,000 in Yellow Nuggets..."

Actually, the initial estimate of the weight of the gold aboard the Portland was underestimated. When assayed, the total weight came in at more than *two* tons!

*The gold ship Portland. Photo used by permission, Alaska State Library - Historical Collections, all rights reserved.*

## Alaska Gold Discoveries

1849 ---- Peter Doroshin, a Russian mining engineer found gold on the Kenai Peninsula's Russian River. However, the strike was almost immediately overshadowed by a gold strike in San Francisco, which started the stampede of '49 to California. Alaskan gold was ignored by most of the outside world.

1861 ---- Buck Choquette found gold on the Stikine River.

1872 ---- Gold is discovered near Sitka.

1876 ---- Gold discovered at Windham Bay south of Juneau.

1880 ---- Joseph Juneau and Richard Harris found placer and lode gold in Gold Creek (a small stream that runs through the center of present day Juneau).

1886 ---- Gold was discovered by Howard Franklin in the 40 Mile District on Franklin Gulch.

1888 ---- Gold discovered on Resurrection Creek on the Kenai Peninsula.

1893 ---- Pitka and Sorresco discover gold in the Circle district. John Mynook finds gold in the Rampart District. Placer gold found on Tramway Bar, Koyukuk Region.

1896 ---- Klondike goldfields discovered by Robert Henderson and George Carmack in the Yukon Territory.

1897 ---- Beginning of the Klondike Gold Rush.

1898 ---- Gold discovered in Nome by the "Three Lucky Swedes" on the Seward Peninsula.

1899 ---- Nome beach gold discovered by John Hummell.

1900 ---- End of the Klondike Gold Rush.

1901 ---- Felix Pedro discovered gold in the Fairbanks area but marked it so poorly he couldn't find it again.

1902 ---- Felix Pedro found a second gold strike in Fairbanks.

1905 ---- Gold found in Kantishna.

1906 ---- Talkeetna gold discovered.

1907 ---- Gold discovered in Ruby District. Gold found on Nolan Creek, Brooks Range.

1909 ---- Iditarod goldfields discovered.

1912 ---- Placer gold found in Chisana.

1913 ---- Gold discovered in Nelchina.

1914 ---- Livengood gold discovered.

### What was it like for the gold rushers?

Very few actually realized the enormity of their pursuit. Some of the early ones died of starvation, so the Canadian authorities required prospectors crossing into Canada to bring one ton of supplies with them. They estimated one ton would be a year's supply and had to include such items as a tent, stove, cooking utensils, blankets, medical supplies, warm clothing and food.

The trails were so treacherous, the journey so difficult, many simply turned back.

### What was the Chilkoot lockstep?

The most famous (or infamous) trail into the Alaskan goldfields was over the Chilkoot Pass. One section was known as the Golden Stairs, and was made up of 1,500 stairs chopped out of solid ice. To reach the summit meant climbing the Golden Stairs as many as 40 times, wearing a 50 pound back pack each trip, until the prospectors entire ton of provisions were at the top. The slow, rhythmic "chorus line" of climbers up the icy staircase was called the Chilkoot Lockstep.

*Doing the Chilkoot Lockstep over Chilkoot Pass. Photo used by permission, Alaska State Library - Historical Collections, all rights reserved.*

### Weren't there easier ways to get goods or supplies over the Chilkoot Pass?

By the spring of 1898 there were three tramways serving the pass: the Alaska Railway & Transportation Company, the Dyea-Klondike Transportation Company and the Chilkoot Railroad & Transportation Company. Some of these trams had buckets with carrying capacity of up to 500 pounds. But there were two problems:

1. The trams could only carry cargo, no human passengers.
2. The trams were expensive, with prices ranging from 5 cents per pound ultimately reaching 10 cents per pound. Since prospectors were required to bring in approximately 1 ton of supplies (2,000 pounds) that could amount to $200! A huge sum of money to carry goods over a pass.

### Why did the Federal Government bring a herd of reindeer from Norway to Alaska during the Gold Rush?

Good intentions gone terribly wrong. Many claim-stakers in 1897 were so intent on reaching gold they failed to eat properly. Scurvy was a common ailment caused by poor diet and lack of Vitamin C. Soon miners began showing up in Dawson City as the first telltale signs of the disease appeared; spongy bleeding gums, bleeding under the skin and extreme weakness. News of miners "starving" began to reach the Puget Sound cities that helped spawn the gold rush. Fearing bad news would damage business the cities and their congressional delegations demanded relief action.

In December 1897 Congress appropriated $200,000 to purchase a herd of reindeer to send to the Klondike to avert the famine. The Klondike Relief Expedition (also called the Yukon Relief Expedition) sent a delegation to Norway and bought a herd of 539 reindeer from Laplanders. The reindeer were then shipped to New York and hauled across country in cattle cars. From there they were loaded on steamers going to Haines Mission and finally driven up Jack Dalton's trail. Along for the ride were 43 Laplanders, 10 Finns and 15 Norwegians to control the reindeer.

Of course the reality was that people weren't starving. There were more provisions per capita than in any years previously. There were just more newcomers who hadn't yet mastered the tricks of proper nutrition.

But there was no stopping Congress. The relief expedition would continue. The reindeer didn't get to Haines Mission until May of 1898 and still had to be herded through swamps, swift streams, snowfields and over glaciers. Reindeer were dying at every turn, taken out by wolves, strangled on their own harnesses or killed by Athabascan Indians curious about tasting the new meat. Many of the reindeer actually died of starvation.

Finally, January 27, 1899, more than a year after the project had begun, the remaining 114 reindeer and herdsmen arrived in Dawson City. The Klondike Relief Expedition had arrived! Of course nobody cared. Those who had heard about it had largely forgotten it and the rest first learned about it when the reindeer were herded down Dawson's main street, followed by colorfully dressed men and women in exotic costumes. In a place where extraordinary things happened every day, this wasn't seen as something too out of the ordinary and was largely ignored.

## What is a sourdough?

During the Klondike Gold Rush the gold-mining camps were very limited on supplies. One of the things they lacked was yeast to make bread rise, so miners would use fermented bread dough. The starter dough for the next batch of bread was saved from the previous batch, eliminating the requirement for yeast.

The knowledge of how to bake sourdough bread was viewed as proof that the prospector was becoming a veteran of northern living.

Miners who survived their first winter were called "sourdoughs" as a mark of respect. The term remains in common use today.

## What is a cheechako?

A term used for newcomers to Alaska. People who have just arrived and not yet made it through their first winter are often referred to as cheechakos.

## What were many prostitutes called who went to Alaska during the gold rush?

"Variety Actresses." While the word "variety" was certainly appropriate, very few would ever appear on stage as an actress. Although, it should be acknowledged many did "act" as if they really liked

men who possess the grace, elegance, and hair of a wooly mammoth.

## What is a troy ounce and how does it differ from a plain ounce?

In America and Great Britain the system of weights used is called *avoirdupois* in which 16 ounces equal one pound. The word *avoirdupois* is from Middle English *avoir de pois*, which means goods sold by weight. In Old French it is *averi de peis*, or goods of weight.

This system is used for most solid objects *except* precious metals and gems. Precious metals are weighed using the troy system. In the troy system 12 ounces (instead of 16) equal one pound.

A simple formula is one troy ounce = 1.097 ordinary (*avoirdupois*) ounces.

## So why are precious metals measured in troy ounces and not *avoirdupois* ounces?

Blame France. In 1527 the troy pound was adopted in the city of Troyes, France as the gold and silver standard. Great Britain was a significant trading partner of France and so adopted the troy pound to make trade easier. The Americans got stuck with it because of Great Britain's influence over the original colonies. The United States Mint formalized the troy system in 1828 when it was adopted for the regulation of United States coinage.

## I've seen gold labeled several ways. How do you determine the purity?

Three ways:

> Percent – parts of gold per 100.
>
> Fineness – parts of gold per 1,000.
>
> Karat – parts of gold per 24.

(Do not confuse Karat with carat, equaling a fifth of a gram, used to state the weight of a gemstone.)

The table on the next page shows some common grades and comparisons of gold.

| Percent Gold | European System | Karat System |
|---|---|---|
| 100% | 1000 fine | 24 karat |
| 91.7% | 917 fine | 22 karat |
| 75.0% | 750 fine | 18 karat |
| 58.3% | 583 fine | 14 karat |
| 41.6% | 416 fine | 10 karat |

**What is the minimum amount of gold that a product can be made of and carry the label "gold"?**

According to the United States Federal Trade Commission *Guides to the Jewelry Industry* the minimum amount is 41.6%, 416 fine or 10 karat.

**Were there really people who made their fortunes overnight?**

Absolutely. In seven hours on Little Creek near Nome, one miner recovered 200 pounds of gold with a rocker box. That's 2,400 troy ounces!

*Sluice box at the El Dorado Gold Mine in Fairbanks, Alaska.*

**What is a sluice box?**

Gold-bearing soil known as "paydirt" is placed into a funnel or box and water is added. The water moves the paydirt down a trough. The trough and box together are called a sluice box.

**How do sluice boxes work?**

Gold is extremely heavy and that weight is used to help recovery. The sluice box has protrusions in the bottom called "riffles." Water is used to wash the paydirt over the riffles and the gold, being heavier, settles to the bottom. If the water is too swift gold can flow out the end of the sluice box. If the water moves too slow heavy rocks and black sand clog the riffles and again the gold washes out. Ideally the water is no more than three inches deep with just enough speed to tumble golf ball size rocks out the end.

**What's the largest single gold nugget ever found in Alaska?**

That depends on with whom you are speaking. There was the 97 troy ounce piece discovered in 1901, the 108 and 182 troy ounce nuggets found in 1903, or maybe it was the monster (called the Alaska Centennial Nugget) weighing 294.10 troy ounces found near Ruby, Alaska in 1998 by miner Barry Clay as he operated his bulldozer. It rolled off the pile of dirt ahead of the bulldozer blade. The record is always being topped, so keep looking.

*In 1903 this was Alaska's largest gold nugget at 182 ounces. Photo used by permission, Alaska State Library - Historical Collections, all rights reserved.*

**How much gold has been mined in Alaska?**

Over the years more than 30 million ounces of gold.

# Engineering Marvels

**When was oil first discovered in Alaska?**

Oil seepages were first recorded in 1882 at Oil Bay on the Iniskin Peninsula, but Alaskan Natives had known about oil for hundreds of years.

The first *oil claim* was made by a gold prospector named Tom White. In 1896 he discovered oil when he accidentally fell into a pool covered with natural seepage at Katalla, about 110 miles southeast of Valdez. After he rinsed himself off he filed the first oil claim. Unfortunately, it would be more than 50 years before a profitable oil well was finally found.

**Whose shoes are bronzed in the Anchorage Museum of History and Art?**

Bill Bishop, the geologist from Richfield Oil who marked where to drill for oil. Bishops heel mark was nothing short of extraordinary. It marked the first profitable oil well ever in Alaska and was the first drilling attempt there by the Richfield Oil Company.

Had Bishop made that mark 100 yards farther away the Swanson River oil well would have been another land office statistic, the 166th nonproductive Alaskan oil well. Fortunately, Bill Bishops boots were made for drilling, and that's just what they'll do....

The entire operation was run on a shoestring budget (that's a pre-bronze shoestring, by the way). In order for the equipment to be brought in to the site, 23 miles from the nearest road, Bishop flew over the area in a Piper Cub with a case of toilet paper. He unrolled a paper trail for the bulldozer to follow from the highway.

In July of 1957 that first well was dug and soon producing 900 barrels a day.

Oil prospecting became so reckless that investors outside of Alaska would purchase land leases without ever knowing where the land was or if there was oil anywhere in the vicinity. One group of Seattle investors actually tried to file claims on a moving glacier.

*Bronzed boots of William C. Bishop. Photo courtesy Anchorage Museum of History and Art, all rights reserved.*

**Is Richfield Oil still active in Alaska?**

Yes! Richfield merged with Atlantic Refining on September 16, 1965. They would become known as Atlantic Richfield Company or ARCO, one of the eight original builders of the Trans-Alaska Pipeline.

**Why is oil so crude?**

You'd be crude too if you were from underground Alaska. Oil can be refined, but it never really becomes polite, and you certainly wouldn't want to bring it home to meet mother. You can take the oil out of Alaska, but you can't take Alaska out of the oil.

**Who is a boomer?**

It usually meant someone who participated in the Alaska oil boom with a pipeline related job but generally had no family, permanent home or other commitment to Alaska.

### What is a cat skinner?

A person who drives a bulldozer (often referred to as a Cat after the Caterpillar Company).

*Bulldozer or "Cat."*

### What is the Trans-Alaska Pipeline System?

A 48 inch diameter pipeline that traverses Alaska from Prudhoe Bay to Valdez, a distance of more than 800 miles.

### Why was the Trans-Alaska Pipeline built?

Because of the discovery of oil at Prudhoe Bay in 1968. The proven reserves of 9.6 billion barrels of oil are estimated to be one-third of the oil reserves of the United States. Unfortunately, these vast reserves were trapped in the frozen north. The most economical way to get the oil out was to build a pipeline to an ice-free port.

When built, the Trans-Alaska Pipeline was the largest privately funded construction effort in history. Construction began on January 23, 1974 and completed in 1977 by the Alyeska Pipeline Service Company. Alyeska was owned by eight oil companies. On any given day the Pipeline transports about one million barrels of crude oil to Valdez. It is designed to transport up to two million barrels of crude oil a day.

### What did Alyeska Chairman E. L. Patton say on March 27, 1975 when he christened the first section of pipe, as it was set underground?

"We are not here to praise the pipeline but to bury it."

### How many people did it take to build the Pipeline?

At the peak of construction, in 1975, 21,600 persons were employed in the effort.

### What did the Pipeline cost?

The original estimate was one billion dollars. The final tab was eight billion dollars. Of that, approximately one billion was used to learn about, combat, accommodate, and otherwise work with the perennially and seasonally frozen ground.

### How many permits did something like that require?

1,347 State and Federal Permits. Hopefully they were written on another 23 miles of toilet paper so they could be of some use later on.

*Trans-Alaska Pipeline. Look closely and you can see Eden Entertainment researcher Daniel Reynen standing underneath.*

### Why is the Pipeline above ground in some places and below ground in others?

It runs above ground wherever permafrost exists. The oil is pumped through the pipe at temperatures up to 145 degrees Fahrenheit. Pumping and friction within the pipe generate additional heat that would have thawed the ice rich permafrost if they buried the warm-oil line. The heat would cause liquefaction, loss of bearing strength, and soil flow. Because of this challenge three types of construction were used. This information was provided courtesy of the Alyeska Pipeline Service Company.

1. Conventional Burial

   Areas where the ice content of permafrost is very low or absent, or where no permafrost exists, the pipe is buried in the conventional manner, as a pipeline is in most areas of the world. About 409 miles of the pipeline are installed conventionally.

2. Special Burial

   In seven short sections, totaling seven miles, the pipe was buried and then frozen into the ground. These are sections that are crossings for caribou and other animals and include both ice-poor and ice-rich permafrost environments. The pipe is insulated with three inches of polyurethane foam covered with a resin-reinforced fiberglass jacket. The temperature of the permafrost is maintained by pumping refrigerated brine through pipes buried beneath the pipeline.

3. Elevated

   About half the pipeline is built above ground because of the presence of ice-rich permafrost. Vertical Support Members (VSMs) are used to elevate the pipeline and disperse the heat. The VSMs are metal tubes filled with ammonia, which becomes a gas in winter and rises to the top of the tubes. In the cold atmosphere it liquefies, running down the pipe and thereby chilling the ground whenever the ground temperature exceeds the air temperature. The devices are simple, non-mechanical and self-operating. Aluminum fins on top of the VSMs permit rapid dispersion of heat.

**What would happen to the Pipeline in an earthquake?**

The Pipeline is built in a flexible zigzag configuration that converts expansion of the pipe into lateral movement. According to the engineers who built it, the pipeline can survive an earthquake up to 8.5 on the Richter scale.

**What country provided the steel for the pipeline?**

Bids were sent out to British, German, Japanese and American companies. Only the Japanese responded and within five months delivery began on the first order of more than $100,000,000 in steel pipes.

**When was the first barrel of oil started down the Pipeline?**

June 20, 1977 oil entered the line at Pump Station 1 in Prudhoe Bay. However, a faulty valve caused an inferno four minutes after the oil started to run. One man was killed and the line was shut down for nine days. The first oil reached the Valdez Terminal on July 28, 1977.

Isaac Asimov in his *Book of Facts* points out that, "At their peak, Alaskan oil wells in the Prudhoe Bay field produced 10,000 barrels per day, as contrasted with about 11 per day from a typical well in the lower forty-eight."

**How many gallons are in a barrel of oil?**

Forty-two United States gallons are in a barrel of oil.

**Why do they use pigs on the pipeline?**

They are devices that go through the pipeline performing various jobs. Dumb pigs clean the pipe out. Smart pigs find leaks and look for damage in the pipe.

*A dumb pig inside the Trans-Alaska Pipeline.*

**How many wells were drilled in the much contested ANWR (Alaska Arctic National Wildlife Refuge) to determine the amount of oil that lies beneath?**

Only one. British Petroleum and Chevron bored into the ground in 1985 on land leased from the Kaktovik Inupit Corporation that owns land in ANWR. On April 24, 1985 they reached a depth of 15,193 feet and stopped drilling after spending $40 million. The well (named KIC-1) was then capped and the wooden drilling platform removed. As of 2002 only British Petroleum and Chevron know what the results from that test site were.

**Are "Tundra Daisys" Alaskan hookers?**

No, and on behalf of Daisy's everywhere, you should be ashamed of yourself. Although, for more information on prostitution in Alaska, see page 24.

Tundra Daisys are empty 55-gallon fuel drums. Thousands of them were abandoned in rural Alaska following World War II and during early oil exploration. When the snow thaws the rust from the barrels gives it a daisy like appearance.

*Alaska Oil Drum...Tundra Daisy.*

**What is the Davidson Ditch?**

A huge project undertaken during the years of 1924 to 1929 to bring water to the Fairbanks area gold mining operations. A company known as the Fairbanks Exploration Company, a subsidiary of United States Smelting Refining and Mining Company, built a 90-mile-long conduit that diverted water from the Chatanika River to hydraulic sluicing operations at Cleary and Goldstream, just north of Fairbanks.

Of course the term "ditch" doesn't begin to do it justice. This was a massive project undertaken before the appearance of the bulldozer when very little was known about construction and maintenance in the permafrost surrounding Fairbanks. The pipeline itself was almost exactly the same diameter (46 to 56 inches) as the Trans-Alaska pipeline (48 inches) that crossed the state many decades later.

Portions of the ditch, including siphons (elevated pipes), can be seen in the Chatanika Valley along the Steese Highway.

*The Davidson Ditch.*

**What is the Marine Highway?**

Alaska's ferry system. It connects coastal communities to the rest of Alaska.

**Are there really "ice bridges" that people drive over?**

Sure are. In the two years following discovery of oil at Prudhoe Bay in 1968 a winter ice road was built from Livengood to northern Alaska. It was called the Hickel Highway after then-governor of Alaska, Walter Hickel. The road was a bulldozer-bladed trail over which trucks drove on the exposed frozen ground and crossed frozen streams. The snow was simply plowed away over the water and the road became known as an ice bridge.

According to eyewitnesses the scariest part was crossing the Yukon River. As a precaution a piece of machinery called a Caterpillar was put in low gear and sent across the river without a driver. The ice cracking sounded like rifle shots but if the Cat made it, the rest of the convoy followed. The Caterpillars weighed more than 50,000 pounds!

Ice bridges are still used in many places in Alaska to shorten driving times in winter where traditional bridges do not exist.

## What is a gold dredge?

A floating gold factory, even larger than a 1976 Cadillac. Gold dredges floated in a pond they dug for themselves. They would scoop up gravel with a bucket chain of giant cast-iron buckets, typically down to the bedrock. The gravel would then be sorted, sifted and washed. After being processed the waste gravel was sent out via conveyor and deposited on a tailings pile behind the dredge.

A gold dredge was first put into operation at Otago, New Zealand in 1867. By 1881 a steam-driven version was constructed and this served as the model for most of the dredges built in North America.

*A gold dredge is five stories tall!*

## Did Alaska really have towns that floated?

That would be the logging camps of Gildersleeve Logging Inc. In business for 80 years, Gildersleeve Logging had two floating campsites at Dall Island's Grace Harbor, Alaska. One was the biggest of its kind in the world complete with a church, school and streetlights. The floating town was taken from one logging site to the next while timber was harvested from the Tongass National Forest.

## What is a cache?

A small log structure, usually a miniature log cabin, built on stilts high off the ground. It is used to store food and equipment away from animals, like foxes, wolves and bears.

*Cache.*

## Why are there electrical outlets at many parking lots in Fairbanks?

They're not for electric cars. On days when the temperature drops below zero Alaska residents plug their cars into the outlets to run a car engine block

*Electrical outlets to plug your car into when it gets really cold.*

heater (battery blanket, oil pan heater, interior heater, and so forth) that keeps the cars warm enough to start. Where plug-ins aren't offered, drivers occasionally leave their cars running during brief stops so the engines won't freeze up.

## What is the story behind the Alaska Highway?

Built in only eight months and 12 days it is considered one of the more spectacular engineering feats of the 20th century. A highway had been investigated as early as 1930 when President Hoover authorized a study of the project. Plans to construct such a land link were rejected by the United States Congress because the War Department had been unreceptive. By the early 1940s the threat of war brought urgency to the need for a continental supply route. Congress realized Alaskan ports were vulnerable to submarine attack and the Japanese were extending their aggressive naval operations in the Pacific. When the Japanese attacked Pearl Harbor, the War Department began plans for the Alaska-Canada Highway.

When construction began on March 9, 1942 it was still winter. Engineer units marched hundreds of miles in 35 degrees below zero Fahrenheit, carrying tons of equipment on their backs. The 35th Engineers marched 325 miles to their station. Within days more than 10,000 men were building as much as eighteen miles of road every twenty-four hours.

When completed, the Alaska Highway bridged 200 streams, more than 8,000 culverts and had employed more than 16,000 workers to build.

## Exactly *how long* is the Alaska Highway?

The official beginning is in Dawson Creek, Canada, (mile marker zero) and ends in Delta Junction, Alaska, 1,422 miles later. Additional sections were built during the original construction including the Haines Cutoff of 160 miles, enhancing the 364 mile Old Richardson Highway from Valdez to Fairbanks (and connecting with the Alaska Highway in Delta Junction) and a connecting road from Skagway, Canada, to Whitehorse, Canada, of 106.9 miles. So *the construction* involved more than 2,052.9 miles, the *Alaska Highway* was 1,422 miles and to go from *Dawson Creek to Fairbanks* was 1,521 miles. Simple enough, right?

## Why did you say the highway WAS that long?

Well, it seems that as the highway is rebuilt and improved over the years, the new road is occasionally shorter than the old one. Alaska state officials thought it would be too expensive to replace all the mile markers and would disrupt the residents whose addresses are tied to them. They left the mile markers in place and travelers just have to put up with the little discrepancies.

## Doesn't the Alaska Highway end in Fairbanks? There's a milepost in Fairbanks that says, "Mile 1523 The OFFICIAL end of the ALASKA HIGHWAY."

Don't believe everything you read. There's a milepost in Delta Junction that says, "Mile 1422 End of the ALASKA HIGHWAY." The sign in Delta Junction is right, Fairbanks...isn't.

*Mileposts in Fairbanks (left) and Delta Junction (right). Both claim to be the end of the Alaska Highway.*

## Why is the Alaska Highway sometimes called the ALCAN?

Before the war Alaskans referred to the proposed road as the "International Highway." However, it was the U.S. military (with its fondness for acronyms) that named it "ALCAN," short for Alaska-Canada. In 1943 the United States and Canada agreed to adopt the name "Alaska Highway" since Alaska was the final destination, but it is still referred to as the ALCAN by many today.

## How much did the Alaska Highway cost to construct?

$138 million in 1942.

*The Alaska Highway. 1,422 miles of rugged beauty.*

## Did someone actually consider connecting Alaska to Russia by private railroad?

Railroad magnate and millionaire Edward H. Harriman did. In early 1899 he financed a cruise and scientific expedition to Alaska. Harriman brought along approximately 60 botanists, geographers, geologists, ornithologists, taxidermists, photographers, scientists and artists as well as his wife and five children. They traveled by steamer that was outfitted as a luxurious floating laboratory.

One of Harriman's intentions was to search out the possibility of connecting Alaska to Russia by private railroad, boring a tunnel under the Bering Sea to link the rails. He quickly realized however that linking Alaska and Siberia, two of the most uninhabited places in the northern hemisphere would be both foolish and expensive.

## Why was Robert Kennicott with Western Union Telegraph surveying Alaska in 1865?

They were considering running a telegraph line overland from the Oregon Territory, through British Columbia, Canada, the Yukon, and Alaska, crossing the Bering Strait to Russia and finally connecting to Europe. Despite the rush to be the first to link Europe and the United States, officials at Western Union Telegraph were happy they lost this race when the first Trans-Atlantic Cable was laid in 1866. Although the Western Union Siberian Telegraph Line would have been an accomplishment of heroic proportions, it would have cost millions of dollars and been impossible to maintain.

Only about 45 miles of line were completed in Russian Alaska before the decision was made to stop work.

## What's the story behind the Rampart Dam?

In 1954 the United States Army Corps of Engineers identified Rampart Canyon as a promising site for a hydroelectric dam. When completed, the Rampart Dam would have flooded the Yukon Flats and created a reservoir the size of Lake Erie. It would have been the world's largest dam, generating more than twice the power of the Grand Coulee Dam.

In 1954 the project was estimated to cost approximately two billion dollars and the reservoir behind the dam would take 22 years to fill.

The Department of the Interior and U.S. Fish and Wildlife Service both opposed the project because of the "enormous losses of fish and wildlife resources." It was estimated that the breeding areas of more than one million water birds and 5,000 moose would be lost. Conservation groups began to speak out in protest as Rampart Dam proposals kept coming forth.

One of the most significant obstacles to building the dam was the questionable need for the five million kilowatts of electricity that the dam would generate. That was simply far more power than Alaskans needed for the foreseeable future. By 1967, Secretary of the Interior Stewart Udall recommended shelving the project. Opposition was getting fierce, the cost was enormous and the need for such a vast amount of energy simply did not exist. Rampart Dam was never built.

**Wasn't there a proposal to divert water from Alaska to the Lower 48 and Mexico?**

That would be the 1964 North American Water and Power Alliance (NAWAPA). NAWAPA projected a shortage in the United States future water supply and proposed the creation of a 500-mile reservoir stretching from British Columbia, Canada to Idaho in the United States. The idea was to move water from Alaska's Yukon and Tanana rivers through a network of canals and tunnels that would join the Columbia, Snake and Mississippi Rivers. The projects estimated cost was $100 billion!

The idea was so crazy one anonymous engineer concluded, "NAWAPA is the kind of thing you think about when you're smoking pot." The project was never undertaken.

**How do people living in the most remote areas of Alaska get messages?**

In many places telephone lines are impractical, cell phones don't reach and satellite phones are just too expensive. So people communicate over the radio. People contact their "local" radio station and leave messages, which are then read at certain times of the day to all listeners. For example: if you wanted to let your brother in a remote camp know his sister just had a baby, you would give the radio station the message. Then the radio station would read it over the airways and your brother, who listens to the messages, would know he's now an uncle!

These radio programs go by various names including the Bush Pipeline, Tundra Drums, Yukon Wireless, Caribou Clatter, Muskeg Messenger, Highliner Crabbers, Ptarmigan Telegraph, Trapline Chatter and Radiograms. Even if you aren't expecting a message it's fun to listen in, sort of like the old party lines only with permission to eavesdrop on the conversation. One ringy-dingy, two ringy-dingy...

**Has the Department of Defense built a device that can open dimensional rifts and be used as a secret death-ray in Alaska?**

Yes, and it's pointed at you right now.

You must be talking about the High-frequency Active Auroral Research Program, also known as

HAARP, located approximately eight miles north of Gakona, Alaska.

First the facts. HAARP is an array of 180 antennas on a land area of about 33 acres. The goal of the HAARP program is "to further advance our knowledge of the physical and electrical properties of the earth's ionosphere which can affect our military and civilian communication and navigation systems."

In a nutshell, there are numerous military and civilian satellite systems whose performance depends on paths passing through the ionosphere. Because many of these satellites are critical to communications systems, it is important to know as much as possible about the ionospheric state as well as what can happen with controlled local modifications of the ionosphere. So HAARP was built as a research-facility, the largest of its type in the world when built.

*The High Frequency Active Auroral Research Program (HAARP) in Gakona, Alaska. Photo used by permission, Air Force Research Laboratory - Space Vehicles Directorate.*

But conspiracy enthusiasts rarely let the facts interfere with a good story. Rumors began circulating almost immediately about a directed-energy weapon, plots to depopulate the Third World, weather modification and a device to enforce the New World Order. But our favorite is a "Top Secret Fax" that was somehow intercepted which talked about the failure of a HAARP site in the Ascension Islands, United Kingdom (U.K.). This is what the FAX said:

*"It has been confirmed as of this date, (01 April 1998) that a failure of the H.A.A.R.P. 15-3 Proteus Unit at Ascension Island U.K. had lost its targeting control during its first operational trial. The*

*accelerator was damaged at shutdown, and will not be operational until 12 June at the earliest.*

*This failure went undetected for approximately 17 minutes, and appears to have caused another series of dimensional rifts along the East coast of the U.S. and Southwest Africa. These dimensional rifts are x-dimensional and have a time frame of –100 million B.C. plus or minus about 20 million years.*

*As was the case in 1995, several predatory reptilian animals have entered our y-dimension and are, as this is written, freely roaming in the Southern New York region, Northern Pennsylvania, West Virginia and a possible sighting occurred this morning at 2:34 hours at Norfolk N.A.S. 150 meters off the beach."*

Of course nobody actually reported reptilian animals…other than the typical political suspects. There are no dimensional rifts and no death-rays.

# Transportation

**What kind of transportation was used to bring people up the rivers?**

One of the more famous modes of river transportation was the sternwheeler riverboat. The riverboat *Nenana* is perhaps the best-known National Register property. It could haul 300 tons of cargo in as little as 3.5 feet of water. Built with accommodations for 52 passengers, it was licensed to carry 16 passengers plus a crew of 35.

The *Nenana* is the only surviving *early* Alaskan sternwheeler riverboat and the last to offer passenger service (1949) and freight service (1955) to interior Alaska river villages. It is the second largest wood vessel in existence today at 237 feet long, smaller only than the 277-foot long side-wheeler ferry *Eureka* in San Francisco.

*The riverboat Nenana on display at Pioneer Park in Fairbanks.*

Today you can still travel on a sternwheeler riverboat in Fairbanks. The Binkley family has four generations of riverboat captains and runs tours during the summer months on the *Riverboat Discovery III* up the Chena and Tanana rivers.

**Do people really travel by sled dog?**

Yes. Alaskan Natives developed the use of dogs for transporting goods and people in winter many generations before Europeans arrived in North America. European explorers and traders recognized the efficiency of using dogs and adopted the technique.

*The Riverboat Discovery III. Photo used by permission, The Riverboat Discovery, all rights reserved.*

**Why are sled dog operators called mushers?**

French speaking sled dog operators used to yell "*Marche!*" as a command for their dog teams to begin. This was misinterpreted by English explorers as "mush." The confusion developed into the tradition of calling sled dog drivers mushers.

**What are bush pilots?**

Pilots of smaller planes that fly into the more remote areas of Alaska. Remote areas are called the "bush" so the pilots who fly there are called "bush pilots." And you probably thought we were going to turn it into something dirty.

**What kind of people rode "wheels"?**

Crazy ones apparently, which would explain its appeal to Alaskans. A wheel was what people used to call bicycles in 1900. It just so happens there was a bicycle craze going on during the Klondike gold rush and at least one company decided to cash in on the popularity of the two. A New York company tried to produce a special "Klondike Bicycle" that would enable the modern prospector an easy ride across Chilkoot Pass, down the Yukon River and on to Dawson City.

It is doubtful the "Klondike Bicycle" was ever built, but many prospectors did bring their bikes to Alaska. One of the more famous trips was made by Ed Jesson who decided to leave Dawson and head to Nome where the gold prospects were better in 1900. He made the entire 1,000-mile trek across the frozen wilderness by bicycle.

### How did Alaskan Native's travel over water?

Kayaks and umiaks. Traditionally, a kayak is a wooden boat covered with skins (like walrus) to make it watertight. One or two openings are left in the center for occupants. The umiak is a wider beamed boat that is open hulled.

### Does Alaska have a railroad?

Yes, but not one that connects with the Lower 48 States. The final spike for the Alaska Railroad was driven in by then President of the United States Warren Harding (also the first President to visit Alaska). He did it on July 15, 1923 in the town of Nenana to commemorate the conclusion of the eight-year construction project.

The entire Alaska Railroad stretches for 661 miles from Seward to the interior city of Fairbanks.

*The Alaska Railroad.*

### What is the snow plow in front of the train called?

A moose gooser, called that because occasionally the plow would push moose off the tracks along with the snow. Their counterpart in the Lower 48 States is the cow catcher.

### What's the story behind the *Exxon Valdez* oil tanker?

The *Exxon Valdez* was an oil tanker captained by Joseph Hazelwood. On the morning of March 25, 1989, at approximately nine minutes after midnight, the vessel experienced a series of "jolts" as it ran aground on Bligh Reef, dumping 240,000 barrels, or 10.1 million gallons of crude oil, into Prince William Sound. This would be the largest oil spill from a ship in United States waters.

Ironically, the Exxon oil spill happened on Good Friday, 25 years after the Good Friday earthquake of 1964, the largest earthquake ever recorded in North America.

*Exxon Valdez tanker circled with containment boom. Photo courtesy of the Exxon Valdez Oil Spill Trustee Council.*

The 984-foot tanker, the pride of the pipeline terminus when it first sailed into Valdez in 1986, had trouble just finding a port for repairs after the oil spill in Prince William Sound. Exxon first considered taking the tanker to Portland, Oregon for repairs, but the Coast Guard and the Oregon Department of

Environmental Quality feared residual oil in the vessel might pollute the Columbia River.

Instead, the damaged tanker entered the San Diego, California shipyard for repairs on July 30, 1990. It was trailing a containment boom and was flanked by a small armada of tugs, Coast Guard vessels and watchful environmentalists in sailboats. The *Exxon Valdez*, renamed the *Exxon Mediterranean*, emerged 11 months and $30 million in repairs later.

Now renamed *SeaRiver Mediterranean* and owned by an Exxon subsidiary, the tanker ferries crude oil among ports in the Mediterranean. It has never returned to Alaska. Senator Ted Stevens inserted a provision in the 1990 Oil Pollution Act permanently barring from Prince William Sound any vessel that has spilled more than one million gallons of oil.

*SeaRiver Mediterranean* is the only U.S. tanker that fits that description. A federal judge upheld the ban. "If I had my way, it would never come back to Prince William Sound," Stevens said in 1990. "There is no lesson learned from a second kick of a mule."

**What did Senator Ted Stevens of Alaska tell the Cordova fishermen who make their living fishing Prince William Sound, before the Trans-Alaska Pipeline construction had begun?**

*"Wernher von Braun, you know, the spaceman, assured me that all of the technology of the space program will be put into the doggone tankers and there will not be one drop of oil in Prince William Sound."*

And the mule prepares to kick.

**What were people called who profited from the Exxon oil spill?**

Spillionaires. Many fishermen were happy to take the oil money since they were making far more ferrying workers, stringing booms and picking up garbage than they would have made fishing.

**How much did Exxon spend to clean up the oil spill?**

It is commonly accepted that Exxon spent $2.5 billion on the cleanup effort but even Exxon critics concede it could be more. Money spent to appease environmentalists and animal lovers included the cleaning and rehabilitation of sea otters. It cost an estimated $90,000 each with approximately 250 otters being saved. More than 35,000 seabird carcasses were recovered.

**How did Exxon figure out the approximate number of seabirds that were killed in the spill?**

By shooting 200 more seabirds, dunking them in oil and tossing them in the Gulf of Alaska and Prince William Sound to see how many would sink. The study was carried out with the full knowledge and endorsement of the United States Justice Department and the United States Department of the Interior. However, both government agencies denied any knowledge of the study until years later in December of 1991.

*Oiled seabird. Photo courtesy of the Exxon Valdez Oil Spill Trustee Council.*

**Does the University of Alaska launch rockets?**

They do! The Geophysical Institute at the University of Alaska Fairbanks founded the Poker Flat

Research Range in 1969. It was the first rocket range in the world that was not government owned, and is one of only five launching ranges in the United States.

**What kind of rockets do they launch?**

Sounding rockets. The majority of them have equipment to study the aurora borealis. The range safety officer, Dan Osborne, clarified the difference. "We launch sub-orbital rockets, not missiles. The military shoots warheads, and we shoot payloads."

One of the other distinctions is that the Poker Flat Research Range has been granted permission to fly their rockets through more air space, over land, than any other facility in the western world. (Mostly because Alaska is so sparsely inhabited and there is very little worry about rockets dropping unexpectedly on unsuspecting people.)

*Poker Flat Research Range. The first rocket range in the world not government owned.*

# Alaskan Natives

**What's the difference between "Native Alaskans" and "Alaskan Natives"?**

A *Native Alaskan* is anyone born in the state. An *Alaskan Native* is someone who can trace their ethnic background to the earliest known inhabitants of Alaska, including the Indians, Aleuts and Eskimos.

**What people lived in Alaska before the arrival of the Russians?**

Tough ones! Who else would live in a place where the temperature could be *minus* 80 degrees Fahrenheit in the winter and up to 100 degrees Fahrenheit in the summer? There were actually three separate ethnic and linguistic groups that called Alaska home when the Russians arrived in 1741.

**Indians** are broken down into two groups. The first are the Tlingit and Haida that typically lived in Southeastern Alaska. The second group are Athabascans who lived in the Interior of Alaska.

**Aleuts** lived on a long archipelago that includes almost one-third of Alaska's coastline and consists of 108 islands larger than a half-mile long.

**Eskimos** occupied the majority of the Alaskan coast from the Arctic Ocean to Tlingit country at Yakutat Bay. The Eskimos' area included Kodiak Island, the Alaska Peninsula and Prince William Sound in southern Alaska.

**What languages do Alaskan Natives speak?**

More than 20! Following is a list of the various languages spoken throughout the state, the areas they were spoken in and some information about the languages themselves. All this information is from the Alaska Native Language Center at the University of Alaska Fairbanks.

## *Aleut*

Location:    The Aleutian Islands, the Pribilof Islands and the Alaska Peninsula west of Stepovak Bay.

Dialects:    Aleut is one language divided into Eastern and Western dialects.
The name Aleut was introduced by Russian explorers and fur traders who conquered the Aleutian Islands and coastal areas to the east beginning in 1745. The historic and traditional name Aleuts have given themselves is Unangan.

## *Alutiiq*

Location:    The Alaska Peninsula to Prince William Sound including Kodiak Island.
Origins and Dialects:  Koniag an Chugach dialects. Russian invaders applied the term Alutiiq to the Native people they encountered from Attu to Kodiak. Alutiiq is the plural form of Aleut.

## *Inupiaq*

Location:    Much of northern Alaska.
Origins and Dialects:  North Alaskan Inupiaq and Seward Peninsula Inupiaq. North Alaskan Inupiaq is comprised of the North Slope dialect and Malimiut dialect. Seward Peninsula Inupiaq is comprised of the Qawiaraq and the Bering Strait dialects. Inupiaq is generally translated to mean "real or genuine person." The plural is Inupiat.

## *Central Yup'ik*

Location:    Between the Inupiaq of northern Alaska and the Alutiiq of the Alaska Peninsula.
Origins and Dialects:  General Central Yup'ik is the main dialect, with four additional dialects of Norton Sound, Hooper Bay-Chevak, Nunivak and Egegik. Yup'ik is both the name for the language and the people. Yup is defined as "person" and pik is "real." The Hooper Bay-Chevak and Nunivak dialects call themselves "Cup'ik."

## *Siberian Yupik*

Location:    Two St. Lawrence Island villages of Gambell and Savoonga.

## *Tsimshian*

Location:    Metlakatla on Annette Island in the far southeastern corner of Alaska.

Origins and Dialects: Tsimshian has been spoken in Metlakatl since the people moved there from Canada in 1887 under the leadership of missionary William Duncan.

## Haida

Location: Southern half of Prince of Wales Island in the villages of Hyadaburg, Kasaan and Craig and a portion of the city of Ketchikan.
Origins and Dialects: Haida is called a linguistic isolate because it has no proven relationship to any known language family.

## Tlingit

Location: Coastal southeastern Alaska from Yakutat south to Ketchikan.
Origins and Dialects: Tlingit is a branch of the Athabascan-Eyak-Tlingit language family.

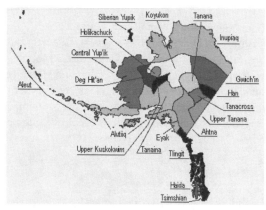

*Distribution of Alaskan Native languages throughout the state.*

## Eyak

Location: Eyak was originally spoken in the 19th century from Yakutat along the southcentral Alaska coast to Eyak at the Copper River delta.
Origins and Dialects: Eyak is a coordinate subbranch to Athabascan as a whole in the Athabascan-Eyak branch of the Athabascan-Eyak-Tlingit language family.

## Ahtna Athabascan

Location: Copper River, upper Susitna and Nenana drainages in eight communities.

## Tanaina

Location: The Cook Inlet area, Kenai Peninsula, Upper Inlet area above Anchorage and coastal and inland areas of the west side of Cook Inlet.
Origins and Dialects: It's an Athabascan language with four dialects.

## Deg Hit'an (Also known as Deg Xinag and formerly known as Ingalik)

Location: Shageluk, Anvik and the Athabascans at Holy Cross below Grayling on the lower Yukon River.
Origins and Dialects: Deg Hit'an is an Athabascan language.

## Holikachuk

Location: Innoko River, formerly spoken at the village of Holikachuk, which has moved to Grayling on the lower Yukon River.
Origins and Dialects: It's an Athabascan language and intermediate between Deg Hit'an and Koyukon. Holikachuk was identified as a separate language in the 1970s.

## Koyukon

Location: It is in 11 villages along the Koyukuk and middle Yukon rivers.
Origins and Dialects: There are three dialects, Upper, Central and Lower.

## Upper Kuskokwim

Location: The villages of Nikolai, Telida and McGrath in the Upper Kuskokwim River drainage.
Origins and Dialects: Upper Kuskokwim is an Athabascan language.

## Tanana

Location: Nenana and Minto on the Tanana River below Fairbanks.
Origins and Dialects: Tanana is an Athabascan language.

## Tanacross

Location: Healy Lake, Dot Lake and Tanacross on the middle Tanana River.
Origins and Dialects: A practical alphabet was established in 1973 but Tanacross remains one of

the least documented of Alaskan Native languages.

### Upper Tanana

Location:    Alaska villages of Northway, Tetlin and Tok with a small population across the border in Canada.
Origins and Dialects: Upper Tanana is an Athabascan language.

### Han

Location:    The Alaskan village of Eagle and in the Yukon Territory at Dawson.
Origins and Dialects: Han is an Athabascan language.

### Gwich'in

Location:    Northeastern Alaska villages of Arctic Village, Venetie, Fort Yukon, Chalkyitsik, Circle and Birch Creek as well as in a wide adjacent area of the Northwest Territories and the Yukon Territory.
Origins and Dialects:  Gwich'in is an Athabascan language.

### Were Alaskan Natives considered American citizens?

Not until June 2, 1924. The Citizenship Act of 1924 made all the Alaskan Natives United States citizens. The act brought almost no aid from the federal government, little education and no compensation for lands stolen. Not much changed until the efforts of Elizabeth Wanamaker Peratrovich.

### What did Elizabeth Wanamaker Peratrovich do?

Helped to pass a law on February 16, 1945 that provided for "full and equal accommodations, facilities, and privileges to all citizens in places of public accommodation within the jurisdiction of the Territory of Alaska."

Prior to that date, anti-discriminations bills had failed twice. Senators spoke in violent opposition to them. Senator Allen Shattuck of Juneau said, "The races should be kept further apart. Who are these people, barely out of savagery, who want to associate with us whites with 5,000 years of recorded civilization behind us?" Senator Shattuck was obviously speaking as the high water mark of those 5,000 years

of recorded civilization. Senator Frank Whaley, a pilot and gold miner from Fairbanks said he "didn't want to sit next to Eskimos in a theater," according to then Governor Ernest Gruening.

When public input was allowed, Elizabeth came forward and began to speak. "I would not have expected that I, who am barely out of savagery, would have to remind gentlemen with 5,000 years of recorded civilization behind them of our Bill of Rights. When my husband and I came to Juneau and sought a home in a nice neighborhood where our children could happily play with our neighbor's children, we found such a house and arranged to lease it. When the owners learned that we were Indians they said, 'no.' Would we be compelled to live in the slums?"

*Elizabeth Wanamaker Peratrovich. Photo used by permission, Alaska State Library - Historical Collections, all rights reserved.*

Senator Shattuck then asked, "Will this law eliminate discrimination?"

Elizabeth continued, "Have you eliminated larceny or murder by passing a law against it? No law will eliminate crimes but, at least you, as legislators, can assert to the world that you recognize the evil of the present situation and speak your intent to help us overcome discrimination."

When she was finished, the senate passed the bill eleven to five.

Alaska now celebrates February 16th as Elizabeth Peratrovich day.

**Do Alaskan Natives worship totem poles?**

No. The totem poles are carved as representations of animals and other beings having symbolic meaning to a particular individual, family or clan of the Tlingit, Haida or Tsimpshian and some

*Totem Pole outside the University of Alaska Museum in Fairbanks.*

Athabaskan Indians. They were never worshipped but served much the same function as heraldry did in Europe.

**Where is a good place to see totem poles in Alaska?**

At the Saxman Native Totem Park. Created when the Civilian Conservation Corps and the U.S. Forest Service retrieved and then restored totem poles from abandoned village sites. Saxman has 24 totem poles and is the largest totem park in the world.

**What was the Alaska Native Claims Settlement Act?**

The settlement of a lawsuit that gave Alaskan Natives money and land in exchange for surrendering their claims to ancestral lands. The lawsuit was one of the last major hurdles oil companies had to overcome before the Prudhoe oil field could begin unhindered production.

The settlement included $962.5 million in cash and 44 million acres to be distributed among seventy-five thousand Eskimos, Indians and Aleut. There was one stipulation. The money had to be given to regional and village corporations rather than traditional Native groups or clans. 13 Regional corporations were set up. 12 represented areas of Alaska and the 13th was for Alaskan Natives who were "at large" or not affiliated with a village.

Native villages were also permitted to organize into corporations but their plans for claim money and land selections were subject to approval by their regional corporations. Under this plan Alaskan Natives could finally control their own destinies but within the legal framework of the white man. It is sometimes called "The Lawyer's Retirement Act" because of the enormous amount of money attorneys made with the settlement.

The corporations and area or region they administer are listed below:

Ahtna Incorporated – Copper River Region
Aleut Corporation – Aleutian Islands
Arctic Slope Regional Corporation – Arctic Slope
Bering Straits Native Corporation - Seward Peninsula
Bristol Bay Native Corporation – Bristol Bay

Calista Corporation – Yukon and Kuskokwim Deltas

Chugach Alaska Corporation – Prince William Sound

Cook Inlet Region Incorporated – Cook Inlet Region

Doyon, Limited – Interior Alaska

Koniag Incorporated – Kodiak

NANA Regional Corporation – Kobuk Region

Sealaska Corporation – Southeastern Alaska

Thirteenth Regional Corporation – Outside Alaska

## What's in Eskimo ice cream?

Berries, seal oil or fat and snow mixed together. In the native language of Yup'ik it is called *akutak*. What better way to cool off on those above-freezing days?

## What is an ulu?

An Eskimo woman's knife, used for skinning, scraping, slicing, dicing and other household needs. Originally made of stone with a bone handle, now most often made of metal and wood. Fan-shaped, it is held at the narrow end by a wooden handle laid across the flat of the palm of the hand.

*Ulu displayed by Eden Entertainment Ltd., Inc. hand model Allen Woods.*

## What is a Billiken?

A small doll sold for good luck. But the origins of the Billiken are surrounded in myth and misinformation. First some of the myths.

The Billiken originated in Egypt and was a symbol of Good Luck, God of Laughter, Happiness, Merry Making and Good Health.

The Billiken originated with the Alaskan Eskimos.

The Billiken is modeled after Buddha.

Nope, no, and no. Billiken have never been found on any archeological dig in Egypt, Alaskan Eskimos carve billiken statues as gifts, but did not originate them and Billiken is not based on Buddha.

The Billiken started with Florence Pretz of Kansas City, Missouri. In June of 1908 she filed a patent for "a new, original, and ornamental Design for Images…" On October 6 of 1908 she was granted the patent and Billiken mania began. The El Horsman Company made more than 200,000 over the next two years as people bought them up across the country. After a couple of years sales dropped off and manufacturing was stopped.

Today, Billiken are available throughout Alaska and sold as good luck charms, many with the phrase, "As a blues chaser, I'm a honey. To bring good luck, just rub my tummy!" A sweet Alaskan charm…direct from Kansas City!

APPLICATION FILED JUNE 3, 1908.

Patented Oct. 6, 1908.

39,603.

*Billiken patent form. Photo courtesy United States Patent Office.*

# Festivals and Holidays

## What are the *Eskimo Olympics*?

It all began with a plane wreck in 1933.

Frank Whaley ran an air service out of Nome. In the dead of winter he took a passenger to the Arctic Slope village of Point Hope. When he attempted to take off for the return flight, his plane ran into a whalebone structure hidden by the snow. His plane wouldn't fly and Whaley was stranded for the next two months waiting for parts.

While Whaley was waiting he lived with the Eskimos and observed many of their games. Those memories stayed with him.

Fast-forward to 1961 and Fairbanks Golden Days celebration. The organizers were looking for "something different" for an event. Whaley was now an executive for Wien Airlines. He traveled to villages on Wien routes to drum up competitors and provided transportation to and from the event. That first year 40 athletes and dancers from Unalakleet, Tanana, Noorvik, Nome, Fort Yukon and Barrow arrived and the *World Eskimo Olympics* were born.

In 1973 the Board of Directors of *Tundra Times* passed a resolution changing the name to the *World Eskimo-Indian Olympics* to more accurately reflect the ethnicity of the participants.

## What are some of the events in the *World Eskimo-Indian Olympics*?

Sports in Alaska are a little different. In order to differentiate from the mundane games, such as the freeze-off, where the last person to lose an appendage wins, the *Olympic* events employ only the highest caliber tests of athletic prowess. Think you're tough? Try competing in some of these events!

**Ear Pull** – a tug of war between two people, with each tugging against a thin nylon string looped around the ear. The first person to give in to pain and let the string go slack or slip off the ear is the loser.

**Ear Weight** – Contestants see how far they can carry 16 pounds suspended from a piece of twine that is looped around one ear. The record is more than a half-mile!

**Knuckle Hop** – Contestants lie on their stomachs and move across the floor by hopping on their knuckles like seals move on land. The winner is the one who can hop the farthest.

**One Foot High Kick** – A competitor must hop on one foot, attempt to kick a suspended sealskin ball with the same foot and then land on the same foot in balance.

**Two Foot High Kick** – Contestants jump into the air, kicking both feet in front in an attempt to hit a hanging sealskin ball. Both feet must remain together from lift-off to set-down.

## Does Alaska have a state lottery?

Not unless you count dating, which is more like Russian Roulette. The closest thing Alaskans have to the lottery is the Nenana Ice Classic. People bet

*Setting up the tripod for the Nenana Ice Classic.*

on the day, hour and minute that the ice will break-up on the Tanana River, at the town of Nenana. The jackpot varies depending on how many people place bets. A 26-foot tripod is erected on the Tanana River and then connected to a clock on shore. When the tripod falls into the river the clock is tripped and the exact time marked.

Originally started in 1917 by engineers working on a bridge across the Tanana River for the Alaska Railroad. They decided to place bets on when the river was going to break up. The first pool was $800. It was later organized in 1959 as a lottery and has paid out millions of dollars over the years.

## What is the Fur Rendezvous? It sounds like a fashion show!

It's actually an annual mid-winter celebration with games, parades, dances, contests and sled dog races. (It should be noted that a party isn't a party in Alaska unless there's a sled dog race.) It is often referred to as the Mardi Gras of the North. It began in 1936 as a fur market and over the years developed into the party it is today. Highlights include the Miners and Trappers Costume Ball, a 75-mile three-day World Championship Sled Dog Race and the World Champion Dog Weight Pulling Contest.

## Where are the World Ice Art Championships held?

Fairbanks, the "Golden Heart of Alaska." Every year Ice Alaska harvests clear ice from O'Grady Pond to be sculpted into incredible works of temporary art.

Ice sculpting began in 1934 when Fairbanks residents carved a throne of ice for the Fairbanks Ice Carnival and Dog Derby. William Graigie and Catherine VanCurler were the king and queen and reigned in fur garments. More than 50 years later ice carving was revived as part of the 1988 Winter Carnival. Ironically, in 1988, the festival organizers had to buy ice from…Seattle…because there wasn't a local source prepared. The ice cost $1,200 and 25 tons were shipped up. That was a bad day to be a delivery driver.

In 1996 Ice Alaska repaid Seattle by shipping ice back to them.

Every year Ice Alaska locally harvests over 1,500 blocks of ice measuring almost four feet on every side and weighing a total of more than four million pounds!

*Ice sculpture Guardian Angel of America by Carl Eady, outside the dental office of Michael J. Helmbrecht D.D.S., December 2001.*

## What is the Sonot Kkaazoot?

Gesundheit. A 50 kilometer cross-country ski race held in Fairbanks every year.

## What is the Iditarod?

The annual 1,000-plus mile sled dog race from Anchorage to Nome. Today the Iditarod is run in commemoration of the 1925 emergency run that brought diphtheria vaccine to Nome, to head off an anticipated epidemic. On the original run twenty dog teams relayed 300,000 units of serum 674 miles, from Nenana to Nome, in 127.5 hours or a little over five days. The modern race is not a relay but an incredible feat of endurance.

**When did the Iditarod race begin?**

The first Iditarod was run in 1967, was 25 miles long and had only a handful of competitors. The first Iditarod comparable to modern races was held in March of 1973 and went 1049 miles to end in Nome, Alaska. Joe Redington, "Father of the Iditarod," organized the 1973 race against hundreds of naysayers who said it couldn't be done. Some of the more interesting things that happened in that 1973 race include:

- There were two, two-man musher teams; that has never been allowed since. The Iditarod race can be run only with one musher.

- The Iditarod was on the tightest of budgets. At the starting line a yellow banner with black lettering was hung that said "Iditarod Trail Race." Anyone who looked at the back side saw the words "Welcome to Nome." Money was so tight they couldn't even afford two banners!

- A packet of berry colored Kool-Aid was sprinkled across the snow to mark the finish line.

- The "Guaranteed Prize Money" was $50,000, an incredible amount for any race but the highest ever for a sled dog race. And Joe Redington didn't even have the prize money when the race started! Fortunately, Redington managed to get loans for all the prize money by the time the first winner, Dick Wilmarth, crossed the finish line, 20 days, 49 minutes and 41 seconds after he started. Wilmarth's check was for $12,000 and it didn't bounce.

**What did Joe Redington do for America's bicentennial?**

In October 1976 he organized the biggest dog team on record, 201 huskies strung out for a thousand feet on Knik-Goose Bay Road. The dogs pulled a bus behind them for almost a mile.

**What does the loser of the Iditarod win?**

The Red Lantern. The reasoning was the last place competitor would be so far back he needed to light his way home.

**Did poodles really run the Iditarod Sled Dog Race?**

Yes, they did! Musher John Suter from Chugiak ran Standard Poodles in 1989. Unfortunately, he was filmed by a TV crew using a spatula to free one of the dogs that was frozen to the ice. The dog was unharmed but the negative publicity eventually led the Iditarod board members to pass a rule limiting the race to "northern breeds."

**Is there a human powered version of the Iditarod?**

The Iditasport Impossible. A human powered race that is 1,100 miles long. The contestants may choose their mode of transportation from ski, bike or foot, but whatever mode is chosen must be used throughout the entire race. This is a long, dangerous race run in the dead of winter. The only thing race officials claim is tougher is going to war.

**What is the nickname of people who enter the Iditarod?**

Ididiots. This is not a race for the sane!

**What is the Pillar Mountain Golf Classic?**

The toughest one hole golf course in America, possibly the world. The "Classic" is held as a charitable fundraiser over two days. The single hole is a par 70 up Kodiak's Pillar Mountain, approximately 1,400 feet high. The hole isn't even a traditional hole, it's a bucket buried in lime green Jell-O dyed snow at the top. PGA (Professional Golfers' Association) rules apply, with these interesting additions:

## Official Rules
## 2001 Kodiak's Pillar Mountain Golf Classic

1. Ball must be played where it lies; a lost ball is a 2-stroke penalty. In a totally unplayable lie, ball may be moved 5 club lengths and no closer to the hole, and player must take a one-stroke penalty. If a ball is buried in snow and cannot be played, it is considered a lost ball with a one-stroke penalty, while ball may be moved five club lengths and no closer to the hole.

2. No two-way radios, dogs, tracking devices.

3. No chain saws, or other power saws; handsaws & hatchets are allowed.

4. Golfer may have only one caddie and one spotter; at least one person in your threesome must be 21 years of age. MUST DRESS APPROPRIATELY! (No hypothermia, please.)

5. No cursing golf officials. ($25 fine.) (yes-we're "serious"!)

6. Take all your own trash off the mountain (including cigarette butts); leaving your trash could result in your elimination.

7. Don't wake up the bears (5 stroke penalty...unless you get away, then we'll subtract 10 strokes!)

*The Pillar Mountain Golf Classic - view from the top of Pillar Mountain. Photo used by permission, Andy Lundquist, all rights reserved.*

Special hints are given including "bring plenty of balls" – you want to have enough to finish the course. Many parts (sometimes all) of the course are snow covered, there are glacier conditions and the winds at the top are strong.

### Where's the official clubhouse of the Pillar Mountain Golf Classic?

Tony's Bar in Kodiak, Alaska, of course. The home of "The worst lies in golf."

### What is an "Iron Dog"?

An Alaskan nickname for the snowmobile.

### What is the "Iron Dog" Race?

The Iron Dog snow machine race is the longest and most grueling snow machine race in the world. Running 1,971 miles from Big Lake through Nome to Fairbanks. Winning teams typically finish the race in under 40 hours and that includes a mandatory rest of 16 hours! The average speed is more than 80 miles per hour. Even races that take place with no real dogs still retain the sled-dog theme.

### What is "Turkey Bowling"?

One of the activities at the North Pole Winter Festival. You've almost got it pictured, but the turkeys are frozen, wrapped in burlap bags and used as bowling balls. No – we didn't make this up! Although one wonders how many frames were bowled before they started using frozen turkeys...

### What is the Mount Marathon Race?

A race held every July 4th up and down the 3,022 foot peak of Mount Marathon, overlooking the Kenai Peninsula port city of Seward. The race is 18,211 feet long and according to credible sources began because of an argument between two old sourdoughs.

Early in the spring of 1915 an argument arose as to whether someone could climb to the top of the mountain and get back in one hour. To settle the argument, a race was held.

Five men entered the original race. The group would start downtown Seward and each could find his own way up and down the mountain. The winner in that first race was James Walters of Seward, who finished the race in 62 minutes.

Today the race goes something like this. It begins with a half-mile sprint from downtown Seward until racers come to a steep cliff face nearly vertical in many places. Then through brush, a nasty thorned shrub called devil's club and over a talus slope covered with sharp, broken shale and slate fragments. Many years a snowfield is present near the top that runners use as a slide in their descent. The final section is a barely controlled free fall to the mountain's base that top competitors can make in eight to ten minutes.

*Mount Marathon overlooking the city of Seward.*

**How high are moose dropped in the Talkeetna Moose Dropping Festival?**

Moose aren't dropped at all. Moose DROPPINGS (turds) are dropped from a helicopter onto a ground target. Each nugget is numbered and sold to raise money for charity. The person who has the number of the nugget that lands closest to the center of the target...wins.

# Plants

## What is Alaska's state flower?

The beautiful forget-me-not or *myosotis alpestris*.

*The Alaska state flower - the forget-me-not.*

## What are "The Dandelion Wars"?

An ongoing battle in Denali National Park. Every year dandelion seeds arrive at the park clinging to the tires of visitors' vehicles. While the dandelion is a common weed in most of Alaska – in Denali it is considered an exotic pest. So every year, when the dandelions are in full bloom, volunteers remove hundreds of pounds of the invading pest to protect the park's biological harmony.

## Is marijuana legal in Alaska?

Only sort of. In 1975 Alaska decriminalized private possession by adults of up to four ounces of marijuana. The laws were expanded in 1982 and several levels of offenses for marijuana possession, cultivation and sale were added. The 1982 changes still had no criminal penalty for private possession of marijuana by adults of up to four ounces.

That all changed in 1990. There was a growing concern over the potency and profitability of marijuana grown in Alaska. An initiative was passed which created criminal penalties for all levels and types of possession.

That changed again in 1998, when a ballot measure passed, allowing persons with medical conditions to use marijuana for medical purposes. That is now being tested in the courts. So technically marijuana is legal in Alaska ONLY if you have a doctor's prescription AND the legal landscape hasn't changed since this book was written.

*Marijuana - shifting laws regulate this plant.*

## Are there any poisonous berries in Alaska?

A few, but one is particularly bad - the baneberry. Incidentally bane is defined by the *The American Heritage® Dictionary of the English Language, Fourth Edition* as "A cause of harm, ruin, or death." Appropriate for a berry that is so poisonous that eating only six berries can bring about increased pulse, dizziness, and stomach pains. Only two berries can kill children. Fortunately, it is so bitter most people would spit it out before swallowing.

## Are there other plants to be avoided?

Cow parsnip or *heracleum lanatum* is certainly one. This plant excretes a sap with the chemical furanocoumarin in it. Skin that comes into contact with the hairs or sap of this plant become extremely sensitive to sunlight. After exposure, if skin is exposed to sunlight, redness, blisters and even running sores can occur. During the summer months, when the sun never sets, this is the perfect excuse to avoid a blind date. "I'm sorry but I got some furanocoumarin on my skin!"

The other would be Devil's Club or *Oplopanax horridus*. These plants can reach heights of ten feet tall and are covered with sharp spines. There are even spines under the huge leaves which break off easily in the skin and can cause festering wounds.

**What plant can supposedly tell when winter is coming?**

The fireweed or *epilobium angustifolium*. This fuschia flower blooms in July and legend has it that when the blooms reach the top of the stalks winter is only about six weeks away. This may come as a surprise to those of you who didn't know winter was ever six weeks away in Alaska.

*Fireweed. When blooms reach the top winter is only six weeks away.*

**What are burls?**

Tumors from trees. They are roundish growths, usually seen on the trunks of spruce and birch trees throughout Alaska. It is still not known what exactly causes them but they grow much faster than their host tree, similar to human cancers. Burls usually don't kill trees but they do weaken them. The largest

of these tumors are used by woodworkers and fashioned into all sorts of interesting and beautiful pieces of furniture and art.

*Tree trunk covered with burls.*

**Where can I find diamond willow?**

A gift shop. Diamond willow is the result of what happens to a species of willow, such as the bebb willow, *salix bebbiana,* when a fungus attacks a branch. The branch dies back as the fungus kills the adjacent bark on the trunk and the layer of white sapwood where the affected branch was. The fungus leaves the red heartwood layer alone and the scar that remains is a diamond shape. Trees that are heavily infected can have diamonds that touch one another and are called diamond willow.

# Animals

**How many kinds of bears does Alaska have?**

Three.

***Ursus Americanus*** or black bear is the smallest. They can also be brown or cinnamon in color (though not flavor) and even blue-gray, sometimes referred to as glacier bear. Its distinguishing characteristics are no hump at the shoulder, the nose slopes straight down from its brow and the creature is generally only 200-300 pounds in size.

*Black or glacier bear. Photo taken by permission at the University of Alaska Museum in Fairbanks.*

*Brown bear with salmon. Photo courtesy Tami Boyer, all rights reserved.*

***Ursus horribilus*** are also referred to as dish-faced bears, Kodiak, brown or grizzlies.

The only difference between a grizzlie and a brown bear is the color – grizzlies have blonde guard hairs.

These bears have been known to reach heights of seven to ten feet and 1,500 pounds in weight. They can run 35 miles an hour. Fortunately, they tend to be shy of people.

Finally, there are ***Thalarctos maritimus*** or polar bears. They inhabit Alaska's arctic regions and can weigh 1,500 pounds or more.

One of the largest ever recorded was over 2,094 pounds. (How exactly does one apply for the job of bear-weigher?) Polar bears are solitary hunters, riding on sea ice in search of prey. They are so closely tied to the sea that they are classified as marine mammals. They have been banned from

*Polar bear. Photo taken by permission at the University of Alaska Museum in Fairbanks.*

73

hunting since 1972 by anyone other than Alaska Natives who are subsistence hunting.

*Thalarctos maritimus* and *ursus maritimus* are two different names for the same bear. Thalarctos is the more recent designation.

### I heard that polar bear hair is like fiber optic cable. Is this true?

Yes, just like your hair is like phone line.

No, it's not true. It all started with some Canadian and Norwegian zoologists, in the 1970s, who discovered that polar bear pelts reflect very little ultraviolet light. That's the light that causes tans and sunburns.

Twenty years later researchers in the Boston area theorized that the hair on polar bears might work like a fiber-optic cable, where light energy travels through the hair to warm the skin. This theory was based on the fact that polar bear hair is transparent. Magazines such as the *Christian Science Monitor*, *The New York Times* and *Time* magazine ran articles about it. Curiously, the theory hadn't yet been tested.

Associate professor of physics at St. Lawrence University in New York, Daniel Koon, decided to find out if polar bear hair really could conduct light. The results were disappointing. Less than .001 percent of red light and less than a trillionth of the violet light transmitted traveled the length of a typical inch-long hair.

Polar bear hair doesn't work like fiber optic cable, and another myth is shattered.

### If the polar bears skin is not absorbing the ultraviolet light, what is?

Penn State University researchers suggest that keratin, the protein from which hair is made, is absorbing the light and preventing the hair from carrying light to the skin.

### What senses does a polar bear rely on?

Polar bears' senses of sight and hearing are similar to humans', but their sense of smell is extraordinary.

Scientists claim polar bears can smell a rotting carcass up to 10 miles away. Kind of makes you jealous, eh?

### What's the story of Binky the bear?

A polar bear at the Alaska Zoo in Anchorage became an unlikely hero when he nibbled on a couple of tourists. It all began in July of 1994 when an Australian tourist climbed over two sets of safety rails to get a close-up photo of Binky. The 850-pound polar bear stuck his head through the bars of the cage and grabbed the tourist in his jaws. The tourist managed to escape with only a broken leg and a few bite wounds, but another visitor caught the scuffle on videotape. The prize shot was of Binky proudly walking the cage later with the tourist's red and white running shoe in his mouth.

That incident spawned an entire mini-industry of Binky memorabilia including:

- A T-shirt showing Binky, the shoe and the words "Send more tourists – this one got away."
- The same T-shirt with the statement "Binky's catch and release club."

### Was that the only incident with Binky?

Amazingly enough, no. Six weeks later two Anchorage teenagers, after a long night of drinking, went for a dip in the pool Binky shares with another polar bear Nuka. According to Anchorage police the teenagers were stripping down in front of the cage when Binky showed up and bit into one of them. The teen was pulled away by his friend but not before Binky had left him with leg injuries.

After that Binkymania hit full force.

- Jokes like "The state won't be asking for any jail time for the kid – it already has its pound of flesh."
- T-shirts that said "Binky for Governor: Take a Bite Out of Crime."
- Editorial cartoons showing Binky talking to his polar bear companion Nuka, "Mauled teen-ager, my butt – how about 'Hero bear prevents youth from drowning?'"
- Letters to the editor of the *Anchorage Daily News* with statements like "When foolish

people place their name on Binky's dinner menu, we should have the decency to allow Binky to eat his entire meal, in peace."

- Another letter asked zookeepers to set aside a day for people to play with Binky. "This program would solve two problems. The food bill for Binky would be reduced and the test scores for our schools would certainly rise."

Now the zoo has erected two strands of electric wire outside the cage and installed a motion detector that blares an alarm. Unfortunately Binky passed away in 1995.

### How can people protect themselves from bears without shooting them?

Pepper spray in a bear's eyes (if you get close enough) is a very effective defense. Just don't spray it until you are faced with an angry bear. It seems that bears are *attracted* to pepper spray if just sprayed on the ground or around tents and campers. It's sort of like a spicy salsa flavoring for them. Also, it should be pointed out that trying to spray it on one's self or another person to keep bears away is a <u>very bad idea</u>.

*BearGuard™ Pepper Spray. A handy accessory when hiking in Alaska.*

### Are there any other animals in Alaska as famous as Binky?

Possibly only Balto the dog. Presumably, you want to know who he is…

On January 21, 1925 several children in the town of Nome, Alaska were diagnosed with diphtheria. Anti-toxin is used to combat it and if not treated in time the bacteria can cause death.

When the outbreak occurred telegrams were sent to the cities of Anchorage, Fairbanks, Juneau and Seward. The only city with any anti-toxin was Anchorage, 1,000 miles away. A train could transport the anti-toxin to the city of Nenana but that was still 674 miles away from the final destination of Nome. Ice flows prevented ships from coming in and blizzards kept any planes away. So, a relay of sled dog teams was chosen to get the medicine to Nome.

Monday, January 26th the anti-toxin was unloaded from the train and given to the first of more than 20 mushers and their dog teams, each relaying the medicine to the next in a desperate race to save the children of Nome. The final handoff occurred February 1st. A musher named Gunnar Kassen took the package with his sled dog Balto leading the way.

Shortly after they set out a blizzard hit, dropping the temperatures to more than 50 degrees below zero and wind gusts exceeding 50 miles per hour. Kassen could no longer navigate and practically gave up hope of making it to Nome in time. But Balto didn't give up. Following his instincts he lead the team through the blizzard and finally arrived, after more than 20 hours, on February 2nd at 5:30 AM.

This relay race became the basis of today's modern Iditarod race.

Balto became world famous appearing on the cover of newspapers all over the world. A short Hollywood movie was even made about him called *Balto and the Race to Nome.*

On December 17, 1925 the sculptor F.G. Roth erected a bronze statue of Balto, the first statue in New York City that commemorated a dog.

## So where is Balto today?

Cleveland, the happenin' place for Alaskan retirees. (It feels like the Mediterranean after being in Alaska.) His fame was actually pretty short-lived. After the initial hoopla he was sold to a "Vaudeville Museum" and used in dime shows and stage acts. In 1927 George Kimble from Cleveland discovered Balto living in deplorable conditions and raised money to rescue him. Ten days later Kimble had the money and Balto was shipped off to the Cleveland Zoo where he was a star attraction for the next six years.

Balto lived the life of luxury (yes, in Cleveland) until he died in 1933 (he was 10). He was stuffed and put on display at The Cleveland Museum of Natural History where he remains to this day.

But that's only part of the story. The *real* hero was a dog named Togo.

## What did Togo do?

A musher named Leonhard Seppala left Nome to meet the other relay participants in Nulato, 320 miles outside of Nome. Unfortunately nobody told Seppala that territorial officials were speeding up the serum run by using a large number of dog teams relaying over short distances. Seppala got only as far as the village of Shaktoolik (170 miles outside of Nome) when he encountered Henry Ivanoff. Ivanoff's team was fighting after trying to take off after the scent of reindeer.

Seppala, unaware of the revised plans was driving past Ivanoff's snarled team when Ivanoff called out "Serum-turn back!"

Ivanoff's team was fresher, but it was obvious Seppala had the experience necessary to take over. So even though Seppala's team had run 170 miles, over the previous three days, he took the serum and headed back for Nome.

## So where does Togo fit in?

Well, Seppala had to decide if he should take a shortcut across Norton Bay and save several hours, or take a much safer inland route. Sepppala chose the shortcut and relied on his lead dog Togo's

amazing sense of direction. Togo led them across the sea ice despite darkness and a blinding storm.

After napping that night in Isaac's Point the next morning the team resumed their journey through gale-force winds and wind-chill temperatures approaching minus 100 degrees. Togo led the other dogs through the storm and completed a 260 mile journey before collapsing in exhaustion 78 miles from Nome at Dexter's Roadhouse, where the next relay team was waiting.

It was Togo who led the dogs through the most difficult part of the race…but Balto who got all the fame. So if you want to see the real hero of the original Iditarod relay, you don't have to go to Cleveland. Visit the Iditarod Trail Committee, Inc. Headquarters. You'll find Togo proudly on display inside the Museum and Gift shop.

*Togo, hero of the original Iditarod. Photo taken by permission at Iditarod Trail Committee, Inc. Headquarters, inside the Museum and Gift Shop.*

## Are there cats in Alaska?

The only one native to Alaska is the lynx *lynx canadensis*, found everywhere in Alaska except the

Aleutian islands, islands of the Bering Sea and some islands of Prince William Sound and Southeastern Alaska. It is a shy animal and prefers to hunt and travel at night. The lynx is more frequently seen in Alsaka during the summer because of the long periods of daylight.

## Are there sea monsters in Alaska?

Only in lake Iliamna. Lake Iliamna means "monument" in Russian and is the largest sockeye salmon producing lake in the world with a surface area of over 1,000 square miles. Native legends state that the monster fish lives part time in the lake and other times in the mountains.

Beluga whales have gone up the Kvitchak River into the lake and it's possible those were mistaken for sea monsters. Another possibility is giant sturgeon, some measuring up to 20 feet long.

## How did the United States Coast Guard end up escorting seals in Alaska?

The Alaskan dating scene left them a little wanting. Just kidding.

It started in the 1890s. Japanese open ocean sealing had reduced the North Pacific seal herd close to extinction. By 1910 an international treaty was signed banning all sealing near the Pribilofs, where the seals had their annual breeding. Unfortunately in 1940 the Japanese denounced the treaty. So an armed escort by the United States Coast Guard began of 2,500,000 seals through their migratory waters to the rocky Pribilof Islands in the Bering Sea. This escort continued all through World War II and into the 1960s. The United States Coast Guard watches over the seals to this day.

## What is the story of Steller's Sea Cow?

First some background. Steller's Sea Cow is believed to be part of the Family: Dugongidae and Order: Sirenia. Their nearest relatives are the gentle manatee of the Atlantic and Caribbean and the dugong of the Indian Ocean, Africa and Malaysia. Steller's Sea Cow is believed to be the only member of the dugong family that adapted to cold water.

Man's first encounter with this gentle creature happened quite by chance in 1741. The ship *Saint Peter*, under the command of Vitus Bering, was wrecked and the crew temporarily stranded. Captain Bering, and many of his crew, died as a result of sicknesses caused by pour nutrition and bad water. For a while food was obtained from the otters, seals and vegetation close at hand. But as time went on this became more difficult. The Sea Cows were noticed and the hunt began.

The *Saint Peter*'s shipwrecked survivors returned home in 1742 and told of their discovery. Returning ships made the Commander Island the headquarters for fur hunting expeditions. These expeditions subsisted on sea cow meat for months at a time. The hunting pressure was so great that the last sea cow was recorded killed in 1768. In an unprecedented 27 years after discovery man had completely destroyed this large mammal.

## Are there Salmon in Alaska that glow in the dark?

Yes, but it's because of a luminescent bacteria. In the town of Holy Cross residents were reporting a strange sight. Salmon hung up in the smokehouses had a "bright glow, shiny-almost how tin reflects in the sun," said Sandra Demientieff to *The Tundra Times*.

"When I rubbed the fish-that's when I really got freaked out because my hand was glowing," Ivan Demientieff added.

It wasn't the result of a sunken Russian submarine or genetic cross breeding. Ted Meyers of the Alaska Department of Fish and Game in Juneau pointed to the culprit, a common phosphorescent bacteria known as "vibro." The bacteria apparently got on the fish in the ocean and traveled with them up the Yukon. Once the fish were hung in the smokehouses the dampness, ventilation and temperature were a conducive environment for the bacteria to grow.

## Do any animals live on glaciers all the time?

Only the ice worm, also known as *mesenchytraeus solifugus*. They are a small worm living in glaciers and can be seen on dim, overcast days or during the hours of dawn and dusk. Discovered on the Muir Glacier in 1887, they measure about an inch in length, may be yellow, white, brown or black and survive on airborne pollen grains, fern spores and algae that grow in the snow.

### Are there snakes in Alaska?

Almost none. Alaska is so cold for so long that most reptiles are unable to survive. The only sightings have been of garter snakes along the Taku and Stikine Rivers in the Southeast.

### If snakes can't survive, are there frogs?

The wood frog *rana sylvatica* is the only North American amphibian living in the Arctic. It's a three-inch frog that survives winter by sleeping through it. (Several members of our editorial team thought this was a pretty good idea.) One of the unusual characteristics of the wood frog is what scientists describe as a "mercy scream" when it's under attack. Scientists don't indicate if the scream works or not.

### Does Alaska have a state insect?

It does. The four-spot skimmer dragonfly as per statute AS 44.09.130.

### You probably thought it was the mosquito didn't you?

The mosquito received 3,035 votes to the dragonfly's 3,914 votes. Then Governor Knowles signed House Bill 239 into law May, 1995. In arguing for the dragonfly, and against the mosquito, Representative Irene Nicholia stated the reason a dragonfly was the better choice, "The dragonfly's ability to hover and fly forward and backward reminds us of the skillful maneuvering of the bush pilots in Alaska." Who knew politicians were capable of such heady intellectual discussions?

### Does Alaska really have a state fossil, too?

Yup. Alaska Statute 44.09.120. State Fossil. The wooly mammoth (*mammuthus primigenius*) is the official state fossil. That's especially ironic since new studies show that it was probably early Alaskans, around 10,000 years ago, who hunted the wooly mammoth into extinction. By that logic, Steller's Sea Cow should be the state mammal.

### What is a fish wheel?

It's a device that looks like a paddlewheel from old riverboats. It uses river currents to move baskets that scoop fish out of the water. The invention originated with the Spaniards, spread to the Indians of the Pacific west coast and eventually to Alaska before the first explorers arrived.

*Fish wheel on the Tanana River.*

### Are there fish in Alaska that can breath air?

The *dallia pectoralis*, also known as the alaska blackfish, can. Its esophagus has evolved to absorb gas so it can survive on oxygen from the atmosphere. In long dry periods the blackfish can even survive in moist tundra mosses until the ponds and swamps are replenished by rain.

### Can't the blackfish even survive being completely frozen?

No. When blackfish are caught some people cover them in a snow pile. The blackfish then mill about under the snow creating a pool of water in the middle where they can survive for many days. This has led to the myth that they can withstand being completely frozen, which is untrue.

### What are candlefish?

A fish also called *hooligan* or *eulachon*. It is a small oily fish. The name came about because when the eulachon is dried you can insert a wick into the fish and it will burn off the oil.

Presumably, the first person to think of lighting a fish on fire grew up feeding seagulls Alka-Seltzer and putting firecrackers in frogs.

**What Alaskan fish hum?**

Sculpins. Biologists estimate that along the Beaufort Sea coast in Northern Alaska, fourhorn sculpins account for more than 69 percent of all fish found. They have some of the most unusual habits of any Alaskan fish. The Pacific staghorn sculpin hums when it's under stress. Take one off your hook when fishing and you may feel the vibration from its humming. The tiny grunt sculpin gets its name from the grunting and hissing sounds it makes when removed from the water.

**Is there such a thing as "left handed halibut"?**

Yes, but it's extremely rare. Perhaps a little background is in order.

When a halibut is born the babies (or larvae) look pretty much like other fish, with an eye on each side of their head. But within the first six months of life the left eye moves to the right side of the fish's head. This allows the halibut to lie flat on the sea floor without dragging one eye in the mud.

A "left handed halibut" is the unusual one in 20,000 halibut whose *right* eye moves to the *left* side of the fish's head.

**What does "working the slime line" mean?**

It means you are on the fish-cleaning assembly line in a cannery. One of the less glamorous summer jobs available in Alaska.

**Do Alaskan flatworms hunt?**

They do. A research biologist by the name of Randy Lamb of Whitehorse found a "predacious flatworm." That's a flatworm that not only hunts but does so in groups. It eats mosquito larvae.

**What's the oldest mammal in Alaska?**

The oldest mammal isn't technically IN Alaska…but in the waters AROUND Alaska. It's the bowhead whale. Biologist Craig George studied bowhead whales for more than 20 years and discovered that some may have lived to be as much as 245 years old! Researchers originally questioned the legitimacy of those numbers until stone and ivory harpoon points were removed from Bowheads that were caught by subsistence hunters. Stone and ivory harpoons haven't been used since before the beginning of the 1900s so finding them placed the age of the whales at over 100 years. Based on studies of the eyeballs it is now believed the oldest whale caught was between 177 to 245 years old, making it the oldest mammal on the planet.

**Do people really eat whale blubber?**

Yes, it's called muktuk. Considered a delicacy by Eskimos it can be eaten fresh, frozen, cooked or pickled. It tastes a little like coconut and salt pork.

**What has ten legs, measures about a yard across with legs outstretched and can reach a weight of twenty-five pounds?**

Alaskan king crabs. King crabs are a member of the shellfish family and are related to hermit crabs. King crabs can live for more than 15 years.

*King crab.*

**What is a musk ox?**

A stocky, long-haired, horned creature that looks like a cross between a water buffalo and a wooly mammoth. It was hunted to extinction in Alaska in the mid-1800s and then reintroduced from Greenland into Fairbanks on November 5, 1930. Musk oxen are now once again found in the wild in Alaska.

*Musk ox. Photo taken by permission at the Large Animal Research Station - University of Alaska Fairbanks.*

### Are there buffalo in Alaska?

Not native ones. Buffalo were introduced in Alaska in 1928. Twenty-three were brought from Montana to a place near Delta Junction. The herd did so well there are now four separate groups spread out from Delta Junction to McGrath and the Copper River drainage. But those aren't the only buffalo in the state.

In the mid 1950s a rancher stocked buffalo on Popof Island near Sand Point in the hopes of establishing a market for the meat. The project never took off but the buffalo did. With no natural predators they continue to occupy the nine-mile long Alaska Peninsula island to this day.

*Buffalo.*

### How about reindeer? After all, if they have the North Pole, then they must have reindeer.

Alaska has herds of them that number in the thousands. But they aren't called reindeer, they're called caribou. Reindeer and caribou are considered the same species. The wild ones are called caribou while the domestic (and red-nosed) ones are reindeer.

*Caribou.*

### What is the Alaska state bird?

The willow ptarmigan.

### What is a puffin?

A colorful, broad-beaked bird that nests in underground burrows and spends the rest of its time at sea. Both varieties (horned and tufted) have orange beak-tips but the tufted is distinguished by long yellowish tufts of feathers that flow back from either side of its head. It is also called a sea parrot.

### Is it illegal to hunt birds with lead bullets?

Sort of. It's illegal to hunt *waterfowl* with lead shot because thousands of birds were dying after ingesting lead pellets in the same ponds in which they were hunted. You can hunt with steel bullets which are more expensive. However many *game birds* can still be hunted with lead. Which leads to the question…if you're using lead shot to hunt *game birds* how do the *waterfowl* know not to ingest the lead?

## How important is Alaska for migratory birds?

Critical. Every spring millions of migratory birds (166 species) go to Alaska from six continents. Alaska supports 66% of the primary breeding populations of the shorebird species found in the United States. 20% of all waterfowl in North America use Alaska's 100 million acres of wetlands for breeding habitat.

## Do people really go snipe hunting in Alaska?

Yes, both real and imagined. The imagined snipe is a joke typically played on shy or quiet kids. The pranksters take their unsuspecting victim to a nearby woods with a gunny sack and proceed to have him or her run around while they "coral" the snipes to run into the sack. The pranksters then abandon the poor victim to make his or her way back home alone.

Contrary to the popular belief however, there really is a bird called a snipe or more formally *gallinago gallinago*. And yes, they really do hunt them in Alaska.

## What's the fastest animal in Alaska?

The peregrine falcon. It's actually the fastest animal known on earth. Peregrines hunt by diving on their prey from great heights. They dive straight down (called a stoop dive) and attain speeds of up to 200 miles per hour.

*Peregrine falcon.*

## Is there a bird that walks underwater in Alaska?

Yes, the american dipper (*cinclus mexicanus*), the only truly aquatic songbird in the world. The dipper can swim underwater and even walk along the bottom of a river, holding onto rocks with its feet looking for aquatic insects or fish to eat. Eskimos refer to dippers as *anaruk kiviruk* which translated means "old woman sunk." The dipper live year round in Alaska.

## What is an oosik?

The penis bone of the walrus, a club-like mass of bone that is often sold in museums and gift shops, carved into cribbage boards or decorated with scrimshaw.

Some oosik trivia you may not know...

- President Nguyan Van Thieu of South Vietnam bought an oosik at the Anchorage International Airport when he was returning to Saigon in 1974.

- The comedian Will Rogers was presented with an oosik in Nome in August 1935. Shortly afterwards he died in a fatal air crash with his pilot Wiley Post.

- Johnny Carson was presented with an oosik on the *Tonight Show* in 1975 by Alaskan Eskimo guests. We believe this was the first time an oosik was ever presented and discussed on nationwide television.

## Do ravens have magical powers?

According to the traditions of some Alaska Native peoples ravens brought the daylight, hung the moon, acquired fire and made the rivers flow. Ravens can be found throughout most of the state of Alaska.

Ravens also have the reputation of being among the smarted birds alive. Scientists have observed ravens engage in complex play and tests have shown the birds possess the ability to learn and solve problems. They even have a form of language. Raven "words" can have up to five syllables and be "spoken" with a variety of inflections. More than thirty different vocalizations have been identified.

**How did ravens disrupt an easter egg hunt in Juneau?**

They kept stealing the eggs! Organizers with the Zach Gordon Youth Center hid more than 1,200 eggs in a park for children to hunt for. Almost as soon as they were hidden ravens moved in and began breaking them open. Many of the plastic eggs contained candy that the birds rapidly devoured. According to Kim Kiefer, Manager for the Youth Center a couple *hundred* of the eggs were stolen. One of the staff members described it as "the most successful disaster ever."

**Are there eagles in Alaska?**

There are more bald eagles in Alaska than anywhere else in the United States. Thousands can be found in all but the northernmost and some western areas of the state. If you're looking for the best eagle encounter head for the Chilkat River near Haines where thousands congregate in the fall to feed on spawning salmon.

Bald eagles in Alaska often attain a wingspan of more than seven feet, and they live as long as 50 years.

*Bald eagles.*

**What were high school diplomas made out of in Fairbanks?**

Moosehide. It was a tradition that ended with the class of 1918.

*Moosehide diploma. Photo taken by permission at the University of Alaska Museum in Fairbanks.*

**Why is there a statue of a dog on Juneau's Marine Park dock?**

That's a statue of the English bull terrier Patsy Ann, the "Official Greeter of Juneau" from 1930 until her death in 1942. Patsy Ann was deaf from birth and couldn't hear ships whistles but would walk to the docks in time to meet every ship. She had no official owner but between ship dockings made her rounds in town for food and a place to sleep. She frequently stayed at the longshoremens' hall.

# Stupid Tourist Questions

### What sound does Prince William make?

Ah yes, the Things that Go Bump in the Night question. It doesn't. Prince William Sound is a long, wide ocean inlet at the northern end of the Gulf of Alaska. Captain James Cook named it in May of 1778 during one of his missions of exploration.

### Is it true that "if it's not hard, it's not frozen"?

That's a myth. There is a tragic story of a man who had a partially frozen foot. A bucket of kerosene was outside in the 40 degree below zero weather. The kerosene was still liquid so it was taken inside. The man's partially frozen foot was deliberately immersed in the kerosene thinking it would be warm. His foot was frozen solid and had to be amputated.

Also, do not believe the myth that "like cures like." Some people believe that you can thaw out a frozen part of the human body by applying something else that is equally cold or colder. There are many cases where a person was just beginning to have frostbite on the nose or cheek and snow was applied to the frostbitten area. The cold from the snow rapidly increases the speed frostbite spreads and the results have varied from sad to tragic.

### Where can I go to see penguins in Alaska?

The zoo. Penguins are not native to and do not live in Alaska. Also, Chilly Willy makes appearances on the Cartoon Network.

### Can I buy wooly mammoth fur?

No. The last wooly mammoth died off around 5,000 to 10,000 years ago. The fur has been out of stock for centuries.

### How do Alaskans protect animals from the cold in winter?

The animals fend for themselves in the winter. Nobody puts them in warm little houses. They do just fine out in the open.

### Where do Alaskans live in the winter?

In Alaska. That's why they're called Alaskans.

### When do caribou turn into moose?

Never. Caribou are always caribou and moose are always moose. One does not "turn into" another. Besides, could you imagine the size of the leftover cocoon?

*A moose emptying out the bird feeder. And you thought squirrels were annoying! Photo by Barry Kier and used with permission, all rights reserved.*

### What are "moose nuggets"?

Those tasty morsels moose leave behind. You're getting the picture. Turds. Poop. Droppings. Clever Alaskans have figured out how to put shellac on 'em and sell 'em as tie-tacs, swizzel sticks and earings. Go ahead and buy some. It gives us jobs.

*Moose nugget tie tac.*

### Where are the igloos?

Alaskans don't live in igloos. They never did. The first 50 times someone asked, it was funny. You don't want to be the 51st person to ask.

### How do Eskimos keep their igloos from melting in the summer?

See question above.

### Why do some Alaskans still wear furs?

They're warm! Don't criticize anyone wearing the fur of cuddly little animals because the harvest and preparation of that renewable resource is much more environmentally friendly than the manufacture of a nylon parka. How do you know it wasn't made up entirely of animals that committed suicide in the wild, in a ritualized hara-kiri?

### When do Alaskans turn on the northern lights?

When it gets northern dark. In other words, they don't. The northern lights are a natural phenomenon and if you ask that question it is an obvious sign you have no idea what you are talking about. But, if you really want to know more about the northern lights (also called aurora) turn to page 13.

### If it's light all summer, how long are the days?

They're still 24 hours long. We just happen to get more LIGHT during those 24 hours than you do.

### If you have the midnight sun, is it dark during the day?

No. The sun remains up until midnight. Depending on the time of year and where in the state you are the sun might not set for several weeks.

### Do Alaskans take American money?

Let's see, Alaska is a STATE just like every other STATE and they belong to the UNITED STATES of AMERICA…Nope. You'll have to exchange your money for fur pelts and moose nuggets. The current exchange rate is whatever you're foolish enough to give up.

Of course they take American money! Alaska is part of the United States and uses the same currency as every other state.

### How much does it cost to mail a letter to the United States?

The same as from any other state. Except in Alaska you have to tip the person in line behind you if they are from Alaska. A dollar is acceptable.

### Will I need my passport to get into Alaska?

You will if you're driving, since the only road to Alaska goes through Canada. If you're flying it's just like flying into any other state. Passport not required.

### Can I drive the Alaska Marine Highway System?

Only if you're in a boat. The Alaska Marine Highway System is a scheduled ferry service for vehicles and passengers throughout southeast Alaska. It is not a road system.

*A ferry on the Alaska Marine Highway.*

### What's the weather like in Alaska?

Are you kidding? What's the weather like in North America? Alaska is so huge that it could be snowing and 20 degrees below zero Fahrenheit in one place and 65 degrees Fahrenheit and sunny somewhere else. Ask the question about a specific city and you are more likely to get a reasonable response.

**How many glaciers are there in Alaska?**

Hundreds. Thousands. A number so large you can't imagine. Actually the United States Geological Survey has named 616 glaciers in Alaska and it is estimated there are more than 100,000 in the whole state. The number keeps changing as glaciers grow and shrink so nobody really bothers to track them all. If somebody asks you, tell them 104,616. And tell them we said so.

*Portage glacier. Just one of thousands throughout the state.*

**Why do so many Alaskans use the same type of incense?**

They don't and it's not incense. What you see are mosquito coils. The coils burn for a couple of hours and repel mosquitos.

*Mosquito coils. Just don't call them incense.*

# Bibliography

**Books**

Alaska Geographic Society *Alaska Geographic – North Slope Now, Volume 16, Number 2*. The Alaska Geographic Society: P.O. Box 93370, Anchorage, AK. 1989

Andrews, Susan B. and Creed, John *Authentic Alaska – Voices of Its Native Writers*. University of Alaska Press: Lincoln, NE. 1998.

Armstrong, Robert H. *Alaska's Fish - A Guide to Selected Species*. Alaska Northwest Books: Seattle, WA. 1996.

Brennan, Tom *Moose Dropping & Other Crimes Against Nature - Funny Stories from Alaska*. Epicenter Press: Fairbanks/Seattle, AK/WA. 2000.

Capps, Kris *The Making of Ice Art – Sculpting the Arctic Diamond*. Wide Angle Productions: Fairbanks, AK. 1999.

Clifford, Howard *The Skagway Story*. Alaska Northwest Books: Seattle, WA. 1997.

Crowe, Ronald *Crowe's Compleat Guide to Fairbanks and the Alaska Interior*. Sundog Press: Anchorage, AK. 1989.

Ewing, Susan *The Great Alaska Nature Factbook - A Guide to the State's Remarkable Animals, Plants, and Natural Features*. Alaska Northwest Books: Seattle, WA. 1996.

Freedman, Lew *Father of the Iditarod – The Joe Redington Story*. Epicenter Press: Kenmore, WA. 1999.

Fuglestad, T. C. *The Alaska Railroad Between Anchorage and Fairbanks - Guidebook to Permafrost and Engineering Problems*. State of Alaska Department of Natural Resources Division of Geological and Geophysical Surveys: Fairbanks, AK. 1983.

Garfield, Brian *The Thousand-Mile War - World War II in Alaska and the Aleutians*. University of Alaska Press: Fairbanks, AK. 1995.

Gray, William R.; Grove, Noel; Judge, Joseph; Kline, Fred; Russ Ramsay, Cynthia *Alaska: High Roads to Adventure*. The National Geographic Society: Washington, D.C. 1976.

Heginbottom, J. A. and French, H. M. *Northern Yukon Territory and Mackenzie Delta, Canada Guidebook to Permafrost and Related Features*. Division of Geological & Geophysical Surveys – Department of Natural Resources – State of Alaska: Fairbanks, AK. 1983.

Matheson, Janet *Fairbanks A City Historic Building Survey 1985*. City of Fairbanks: Fairbanks, AK. 1985.

Mighetto, Lisa and Homstad, Carla *Engineering in the Far North - A History of the U.S. Army Engineer District in Alaska*. Historical Research Associates, Inc: Missoula, MT. 1997.

Milepost Editors *Alaska A to Z*. Vernon Publications Inc.: Bellevue, WA. 1997.

Milepost Editors *Alaska Wilderness Milepost*. Alaska Northwest Books: Bothell, WA 1990.

Morgan, Lael *Alaska's Native People*. Alaska Geographic Society, Volume 6, Number 3: Anchorage, AK. 1979.

Naske, Claus-M and Blohm, Hans *Alaska*. Skyline Press/Oxford University Press (Canadian Branch): Toronto, Canada. 1985.

Naske, Claus-M and Slotnick, Herman E. *Alaska - A History of the 49th State Second Edition*. University of Oklahoma Press: Norman, OK. 1994.

Naske, Claus-M and Rowinski, Ludwig J. *Fairbanks - a pictorial history*. The Donning Company/Publishers: Norfolk, VA. 1981.

O'Haire, Daniel and Connor, Cathy *Roadside Geology of Alaska*. Mountain Press Publishing Company: Missoula, MT. 1988.

O'Meara, Jan *Alaska Dictionary and Pronunciation Guide.* Wizard Works, Jan O'Meara: Homer, AK. 1988.

Reger, R. D. and Péwé, Troy L. *Guidebook to Permafrost and Quaternary Geology along the Richardson and Glenn Highways between Fairbanks and Anchorage, Alaska.* Alaska Division of Geological and Geophysical Surveys: Fairbanks, AK. 1983.

Rennick, Penny *Alaska Geographic – Alaska's Weather The Quarterly / Volume 18, Number 1.* The Alaska Geographic Society: Anchorage, AK. 1991.

Ritter, Harry *Alaska's History - The People, Land, and Events of the North Country.* Alaska Northwest Books: Seattle, WA. 1993.

Rudd, Sandra and Brown, Tricia *The Alaska Almanac Facts About Alaska 23rd Edition.* Alaska Northwest Books: Seattle, WA. 1999.

Satterfield, Archie *The Most Famous Trail in the North Chilkoot Pass - A Hiker's Historical Guide to the Klondike Gold Rush National Historical Park.* Alaska Northwest Books: Seattle, WA. 1998.

Schaff, Ross G. and Péwé, Troy L. *Geologic Hazards of the Fairbanks Area, Alaska – Special Report 15.* Division of Geological & Geophysical Surveys: College, AK. 1982.

Sherwonit, Bill *Iditarod - The Great Race to Nome.* Sasquatch Books: Seattle, WA. 2002.

Spezialy, Millie *Binky's Trophy.* Six Suns Publishing Company: Anchorage, AK. 1996.

Stefánsson, Vilhjálmur *Unsolved Mysteries of the Arctic.* Press North America: Sunnyvale, CA. 1938.

Strohmeyer, John *Extreme Conditions – Big Oil and the Transformation of Alaska.* Cascade Press: Anchorage, AK. 1997.

Taylor, Alan *The Strangest Town in Alaska - The History of Whittier, Alaska and the Portage Valley.* Kokogiak Media: Seattle, WA. 2000.

Wendt, Ron *Alaska Gold Prospectors Guide.* Goldstream Publications: Wasilla, AK. 1995.

Wendt, Ron *Strange, Amazing! True Tales of Alaska!:* Goldstream Publications: Wasilla, AK. 1995.

Wheeler, Keith *The Old West – The Alaskans:* Time Life Books: Alexandria, VA. 1977.

Whisenhant, James *Wildlife of Alaska:* James Whisenhant: Fairbanks, AK. 1976.

*World Ice Art Championships – Ice Art 2000.* Ice Alaska, Inc.: Fairbanks, AK. 2000.

Zimmerman, Steven and Hood, Donald *The Gulf of Alaska – Physical Environment and Biological Resources.* Alaska Office, Ocean Assessments Division, National Oceanic and Atmospheric Administration, U.S. Department of Commerce with financial support from the Alaska OCS Region Office, Minerals Management Service, U.S. Department of the Interior: Washington, D.C. 1986.

Zuehkle, Mark *The Yukon Fact Book.* Whitecap Books: Vancouver/Toronto, Canada. 1998.

## Magazines - Newspapers

*Alaska Science Forum,* Big Splashes in a Little Bay – Article #763, Larry Gedney, April 7, 1986.

*Alaska Science Forum,* Rock Glaciers – Article #251, T. Neil Davis, September 7, 1978.

*Alaska Science Forum,* Temperature Trivia for the Mercury-Addicted – Article #1322, Ned Rozell, July 27, 1995.

*Alaska Science Forum,* The Wanderings of the Arctic Circle – Article #1349, Ned Rozell, August 7, 1997.

*Alaska – The Magazine of Life on the Last Frontier,* Alaska Disaster, A Short History of a Tragedy, Ronald L. Lautaret, November 1999.

*Alaska – The Magazine of Life on the Last Frontier,* The Alaska Sportsman, Confessions of an Iditarod Rookie, Edited by Ken Marsh, March 1990.

*Alaska – The Magazine of Life on the Last Frontier,* Bird Bandits, Sherry Simpson, Juneau Empire, April 1992.

*Alaska – The Magazine of Life on the Last Frontier,* The Bungled Bingle Caper, Ketchikan to Barrow Remembrances, Naomi Warren Klouda, October 1991.

*Alaska – The Magazine of Life on the Last Frontier,* The Christmas Place – North Pole, Alaska…where the sacred and the secular live in peace, Catherine Stadem, December/January 1996.

*Alaska – The Magazine of Life on the Last Frontier,* City in Silence, George Herben, June 1989.

*Alaska – The Magazine of Life on the Last Frontier,* The Great One at a Glance, November 1990.

*Alaska – The Magazine of Life on the Last Frontier,* "Left-Handed" Halibut, May/June 1994.

*Alaska – The Magazine of Life on the Last Frontier,* Malaspina Melting, But it's Still Bigger Than Rhode Island, Ned Rozell, April 2000.

*Alaska – The Magazine of Life on the Last Frontier,* Mystery of the Igloo, February 1994.

*Alaska – The Magazine of Life on the Last Frontier,* Patsy Ann's Dogged Spirit, Waiting on the Juneau Dock, May/June 1993.

*Alaska – The Magazine of Life on the Last Frontier,* Paying for the Past, March 2001.

*Alaska – The Magazine of Life on the Last Frontier,* Polar Bear Hair Myth Exposed – Popular Legend Disproven, Ned Rozell, Alaska Science Forum, September 1998.

*Alaska – The Magazine of Life on the Last Frontier,* Seward's Fabulous Folly, Bill Sherwonit, July 1994.

*Alaska – The Magazine of Life on the Last Frontier,* Spice Bears, Pepper Spray May Attract, Not Repel, May/June 1998.

*Alaska – The Magazine of Life on the Last Frontier,* Quote Page 12, April 1993.

*Alaska – The Magazine of Life on the Last Frontier,* The Virtual (Arctic) Circle, February 1997.

*Alaska – The Magazine of Life on the Last Frontier,* What Goes Up Must Chow Down, Climbers Watch their Weight on Denali's 'Fat Farm', T. Massari McPherson, May/June 1994.

*Alaska – The Magazine of Life on the Last Frontier,* Where Buffalo Roam, January 1992.

*Alaska Journal – History and Arts of the North,* From Dawson to Nome on a Bicycle, Volume 15, Number 1, Edward R. Jesson, Winter 1985.

*Alaska Journal – History and Arts of the North,* A One Horse Town, Volume 15, Number 1, Charlie Jones, Winter 1985.

*Earthquakes – The Next Big Earthquake in Southern Alaka may Come Sooner Than You Think,* Alaska Earthquake Statistics, U.S. Geological Survey, Distributed by local Alaska Newspapers.

*Fairbanks Daily News-Minor,* Ad for lead shells is way off target, Tim Mowry, Friday, May 4, 2001.

*Fairbanks Daily News-Minor,* Anchorage-area team tops Iron Dog, Amanda Bohman, Sunday, February 25, 2001.

*Fairbanks Daily News-Minor,* Assembly bans new outhouses in urban areas, Amanda Bohman, Friday, June 15, 2001.

*Fairbanks Daily News-Minor,* Bill nixes firearm requirement from pilot's emergency gear, The Associated Press, Sunday, April 29, 2001.

*Fairbanks Daily News-Minor,* Everybody wants to know the secret of test well KIC-1, Joseph B. Verrengia, Sunday, April 8, 2001.

*Fairbanks Daily News-Minor,* Keck Effect shows light poles bend in March weather, Dermot Cole, Tuesday, March 20, 2001.

*Fairbanks Daily News-Minor,* Men-women gap closing in Alaska, Maureen Clark, Tuesday, May 22, 2001.

*Fairbanks Daily News-Minor,* Nenana tripod ready to take the plunge, Diana Campbell, Monday, March 5, 2001.

*Fairbanks Daily News-Minor*, Snowmachine laws unlikely despite risks, Dan Joling, Sunday, February 11, 2001.

*Fairbanks Daily News-Minor*, Sonot Kkaazoot punishes even its victorious skiers, Amy Miller, Sunday, March 25, 2001.

*Golden Valley,* Reaching for the aurora, Debbie S. Miller, October 1990.

*Heartland,* (Page H-6) Bowhead whale may be oldest mammal, Ned Rozell, February 25, 2001.

*Heartland,* (Page H-2) Dandelion wars to resume in Denali, April 8, 2001.

*Heartland,* (Page H-14) Debunking the myth of polar bear hair, Ned Rozell, May 13, 1998.

*Heartland,* (Page H-6) Deceiving is believing in the North, Sherry Simpson March 27, 1988.

*Heartland,* (Page H-6) Field Sketches: Return of the Wanderers, Mark D. Ross, April 22, 2001.

*Heartland,* (Page H-9) Milestones on the mountain, May 13, 2001.

*Heartland,* (Page H-4) Native Olympics sport tradition, Debbie Carter, July 28, 1985.

*Heartland,* (Page H-3) Poles in peril, April 8, 2001.

*Heartland,* (Page H-4) Unknown legacy of Alaska's atomic tests, Ned Rozell, January 28, 2001.

*National Geographic,* (Volume 164, No. 3) Alaska's Far-Out Islands – The Aleutians, Lael Morgan, September, 1983.

*National Geographic,* (Volume 195, No. 3) In the Wake of the Spill – Ten years After Exxon Valdez, John G. Mitchell, March, 1999.

*National Parks – The Magazine of The National Parks Conservation Association,* Nanuuq of the North, Bill Sherwonit, September/October 2001.

**Museums - Institutes**

Alaska Native Heritage Center
8800 Heritage Center Drive
Anchorage, Alaska 99506

Alaska SeaLife Center
301 Railway Avenue
P.O. Box 1329
Seward, AK 99664

Alaska State Museum
395 Whittier St.
Juneau, AK 99801-1718

Anchorage Museum of History and Art
121 West Seventh Avenue
Anchorage, AK 99501

Cleveland Museum of Natural History,
1 Wade Oval Drive, University Circle
Cleveland, Ohio 44106-1767

Iditarod Trail Sled Dog Race
Mile 2.2 Knik Road
Wasilla, AK 99654

Mushers' Hall of Fame
Mile 13.9 Knik Road
Wasilla, AK 99654

Sheldon Jackson Museum
104 College Drive
Sitka, AK 99835-7657

University of Alaska Museum
907 Yukon Drive
Fairbanks, AK 99775

**Internet Resources**

50 States.com – States and Capitals [Weber Publications] http://www.50states.com/ last accessed 11/21/2000.

Alaska's Best – Attractions [Alaska's Best] http://www.alaskasbest.com/attract.htm last accessed 7/22/2001.

An Integrated Approach for Monitoring Changes at Bering Glacier, Alaska by [Bruce F. Molnia, U.S. Geological Survey, Reston, VA 22092 Austin Post, U.S. Geological Survey (Retired), Vashon, WA. 98070] http://chht-ntsrv.er.usgs.gov/Glacier_wkshp/bering.htm last accessed 12/05/2000.

Alaska Native Language Center, by [University of Alaska Fairbanks, Alaska Native Language

Center – Fairbanks AK] http://www.uaf.edu/anlc/ last accessed 8/29/2001.

Camera Workers: The British Columbia Photographic Directory, 1858-1950 - W - Volume 1 (1858-1900) by [David Mattison] http://members.home.net/historian/cw1-w-names.html last accessed 12/07/2000.

Gildersleeve Logging, Inc: End of an Era: Gildersleeve logging camps close, by [Tom Miller] Daily News Staff Writer, Ketchikan Newspaper. http://www.gildersleevelogging.com/ last accessed 8/10/2001.

Iditasport Impossible: The Iditarod Trail to Nome Home Page, http://www.iditasport.com/impossible/index.html last accessed 7/15/2001.

Katmai and Novarupta, Alaska Peninsula, Alaska [Volcano World] http://volcano.und.nodak.edu/vwdocs/volc_images/north_america/alaska/katami.html last accessed 12/12/2000.

MALASPINA GLACIER, ALASKA Plate G-7 Geomorphology from Space [NASA (National Aeronautics & Space Administration) Johnson Space Center] http://daac.gsfc.nasa.gov/DAAC_DOCS/geomorphology/GEO_9/GEO_PLATE_G-7.HTML last accessed 12/05/2000.

Northern Light, The – Features – Civil Rights Heroine, The Story of Elizabeth Peratrovich [Susan Pierce UAA Student] http://www.uaa.alaska.edu/light/march27/features8.htm last accessed 7/23/2001.

Peregrine biology: NATURAL HISTORY [The Canadian Peregrine Foundation] http://www.peregrine-foundation.ca/info/biology.html last accessed 11/16/2000.

Pillar Mountain Golf Classic [Professional Cross Country Golfers Association and Tony's Bar of Kodiak Alaska] http://www.kodiak.org/pillar/pillar.html last accessed 1/10/2001.

Pioneers of Alaska [Pioneers of Alaska Auxiliary No. 8] http://www.ptialaska.net/~fgs/research/clubs/pioneers.htm last accessed 7/16/2001.

State Population Estimates and Demographic Components of Population Change: July 1, 1998 to July 1, 1999 [The United States Census Bureau] http://www.census.gov/population/estimates/state/st-99-1.txt last accessed 11/21/2000.

University of Alaska Geophysical Institute in Fairbanks The Great Gorge at Mount McKinley is Deeper than the Grand Canyon by [Science Editor-in-Chief Kathy Berry] http://www.gi.alaska.edu/GI_front_page/InfoOffice/gorge.html last accessed 8/11/2001.

World Eskimo-Indian Olympics [WEIO - World Eskimo-Indian Olympics (aka World Exhibition of Indigenous Olympics)] http://www.weio.org/ last accessed 7/27/2002.

# Index

## S

## V

## W

## X

## Y

## Z